From Text
to Epitext

From Text to Epitext

*Expanding Students'
Comprehension, Engagement,
and Media Literacy*

Shelbie Witte, Melissa Gross,
and Don Latham, Editors

Foreword by Teri S. Lesesne

**LIBRARIES
UNLIMITED**®

An Imprint of ABC-CLIO, LLC

Santa Barbara, California • Denver, Colorado

Library of Congress Cataloging-in-Publication Data

Names: Witte, Shelbie, editor. | Gross, Melissa, editor. | Latham, Don, 1959– editor.
Title: Text to epitext : expanding students' comprehension, engagement, and media literacy / Shelbie Witte, Melissa Gross, and Don Latham, editors ; foreword by Teri S. Lesesne.
Description: Santa Barbara, California : Libraries Unlimited, an Imprint of ABC-CLIO, LLC, [2021] | Includes bibliographical references and index.
Identifiers: LCCN 2020033681 (print) | LCCN 2020033682 (ebook) | ISBN 9781440877490 (paperback) | ISBN 9781440877506 (ebook)
Subjects: LCSH: Reading comprehension. | Critical thinking. | Media literacy.
Classification: LCC LB1573.7 .T49 2021 (print) | LCC LB1573.7 (ebook) | DDC 372.47—dc23
LC record available at https://lccn.loc.gov/2020033681
LC ebook record available at https://lccn.loc.gov/2020033682

ISBN: 978-1-4408-7749-0 (print)
      978-1-4408-7750-6 (ebook)

25 24 23 22 21   1 2 3 4 5

This book is also available as an eBook.

Libraries Unlimited
An Imprint of ABC-CLIO, LLC

ABC-CLIO, LLC
147 Castilian Drive
Santa Barbara, California 93117
www.abc-clio.com

This book is printed on acid-free paper ∞

Manufactured in the United States of America

Contents

Foreword

Teri S. Lesesne

If, like me, you were not familiar with the term *epitext*, you are not alone. When asked to write this introduction, I dove into a little research about the term. As I read through chapters by Jim Blasingame, Sharon Kane, Stephanie Toliver, and W. Kyle Jones, my preliminary knowledge of epitext expanded from books to film and television. Being able to refer to a variety of media assists readers in identifying examples of epitext, how it is used in a variety of media, and what knowledge is gleaned from identifying its use, effects, and influences.

The advent of the Common Core State Standards (CCSS) changed much of educators' focus on prereading strategies such as providing background knowledge and noting vocabulary that might be difficult during reading. Instead, David Colemean, the architect of CCSS, discussed a significant change when approaching a text. Coleman defined the questions teachers should ask as "text dependent" (Coleman, 2011). This paradigm shift (Coleman's words, not mine) required readers to stay within the four corners of a text. Imagine for just a moment what all readers might lose if educators followed this shift. That is, in part, what this insightful book tackles with its discussion of the importance of epitext.

Many authors share inspirations, back stories, and more. As I write this foreword during the coronavirus pandemic, dozens of authors are offering conversations about their writing in online presentations. Children's and YA authors provide examples of epitext for readers of all ages. Information might also be found in interviews with authors, on publisher websites, and even on some blogs that discuss the work of authors, Tidbits about the authors and the books are not the only examples of epitext.

When I was teaching eighth-graders, we had the good fortune of doing a phone interview with the grande dame of YA mysteries from the 1980s, Joan Lowery Nixon. Most of my students had read one of her mysteries, most selecting *Whispers from the Dead* because it was set in Houston. Nixon talked about the inspiration for the book. After the call, those students who had already read the book—and many who had not read it yet—wanted a copy of her book. Students wanted to see if they could track the "reality" of the novel.

Anyone who was fortunate enough to hear author Robert Cormier speak knew the backstory of *The Chocolate War*. Patty Campbell, author and YA critic, penned a column for *The Horn Book* called "The Sand in the

Oyster." She focused on that tiny grain of sand that the oyster coats again and again to end the irritation. The end result is a beautiful pearl. For Robert Cormier, the grain was his son announcing that he did not want to participate in the schoolwide candy sale. Cormier assured his son that it was fine for him not to participate, but then that grain began to irritate: what would happen if it were *not* okay? That "what if" question was the sand in the oyster that eventually became a beautiful pearl.

It is important to note that a great deal of discussion of epitexts can occur before the actual reading of the book. In the interest of allowing students choice in reading material, after some practice, students can identify the epitexts they notice for their individual books. Chapters in this book deal with fiction and nonfiction as well as different forms and formats (e.g., graphic novels, picture books), which will provide plentiful examples for some mini-lessons and then independent practice for students. Utilized before the reading, epitexts can become instances of prediction; used after reading takes place, epitexts work wonderfully as reflection points. Information about the author, such as previous works, interviews, biographical publications, Skype and school visits, and even author photographs, can function as epitext. Additionally, another author's recommendation might serve to entice a reader. There is almost no limit to epitexts as educators either begin the approach to the text or begin the post-reading discussion of the book.

The various chapters in this book provide information, both pedagogical and practical, about epitexts. Examples from different genres and subgenres, different forms, and different media make a clear-cut case for using epitext to deepen reading and response to reading. Rather than narrowing reading to the four corners of the text as Coleman suggested years ago, readers can stretch beyond the confines of the page using epitexts. Not to do so would mean losing so much more than the four corners on their own might offer.

Introduction: The Functions of Epitext

Shelbie Witte, Don Latham, and Melissa Gross

Whenever we encounter a text, we do so within a particular context. The context is personal—one's own background, experiences, and beliefs—and also societal—society's ways of looking at, thinking about, and talking about a text. Thus, the context for any text is, to say the least, complicated. A useful framework for considering context is provided by Gérard Genette's concept of paratext. In *Paratexts: Thresholds of Interpretation* (1997), Genette describes *paratext* as those elements surrounding a text, pointing both inward toward the text and outward "toward the world's discourse about the text" (p. 2). The paratext serves as a "threshold" or a "'vestibule' that offers the world at large the possibility of either stepping inside [the text] or turning back" (p. 2). As Genette conceives of it, the paratext is comprised of two main parts. *Peritext* refers to those elements that are part of the same text but are not part of the text proper. For example, peritextual elements of a book include such things as the dust jacket, the title page, the table of contents, the afterword, the references, the index, and so forth. The other main part of the paratext is what Genette calls *epitext*, which he defines as those elements that are outside of the volume itself but are closely connected to the text. Epitextual elements include such things as communications between the author and editor, advertising for the text, interviews with the author, the author's website, reviews of the text, literary criticism focused on the text, and so on.

Though Genette discusses the functions of various specific paratextual elements, he does not group these functions into categories. Gross and Latham (2017) have taken this additional step and organized peritextual elements into six functional categories:

1. Production (e.g., title, author, publisher)

2. Promotional (e.g., blurb, author biography, excerpts from reviews, award medallions)

3. Navigational (e.g., table of contents, index)

4. Intratextual (e.g., foreword, dedication, author's note)

5. Supplemental (e.g., glossary, maps, timeline)

6. Documentary (e.g., bibliography, image credits, source notes, suggested reading).

Although Genette focuses on books (and the examples presented here are book-focused as well), the concept of peritext can be applied across media. The Production elements of a film, for instance, would include the director's name and the names of the producers. The Supplemental elements of the DVD version of a film might include a track with additional commentary by the actors. These elements are not the film per se, but are instead packaged with the film. Peritextual elements help to provide context by offering information about when and how a work was created, by whom, and for what purpose. A wide range of applications of the Peritextual Literacy Framework within the classroom and/or library in PK-20 contexts can be found in *Literacy Engagement Through Peritextual Analysis* (Witte, Latham, & Gross, 2019).

Epitext

The *epitext*, made up of those elements not bound to the physical manifestation of a work, is arguably an even richer source for contextual information about the work. Genette (1997) discusses two main types of epitext: the public, i.e., those elements that are intended from the outset to be seen by the public at large; and the private, those elements that are initially intended to be seen by only a few people, perhaps even only by the author. A published interview with the author about a particular work would be an example of public epitext connected to that work. An author's journal that contains entries related to ideas for the work would be an example of private epitext (although the journal, or portions of it, might later be published and thus become public epitext).

As with peritext, Genette does not define functional categories of epitext, but based on his discussion and the examples he provides, such categories can be readily formulated.

Production epitext is those elements that relate to the production of a text. These elements include author correspondence about the gestation of the text, outlines, drafts, storyboards, author journals and diaries, page proofs, corrections, and the like. Useful questions for considering production epitext are:

- What do these elements tell you about the work?

- What do they tell you about how the work was created?

- What sources and/or experiences provided inspiration for the work?

Promotion epitext is elements related to the promotion and marketing of a text. Promotion elements can include advertisements (print, online), posters, flyers, trailers, previews, and so on. Useful questions for considering promotion epitext are:

- What do these elements tell you about the work's content?

- How do they attempt to make the work appealing?

- What do they tell you about the intended audience for the work?

- Are these elements an accurate reflection of the work itself?

- How do these elements affect your view of the work?

- Are these elements interesting? Convincing? Effective? Why or why not?

Dissemination epitext is elements related to the sharing and widespread dissemination of a work. Closely related to promotion, these elements might be thought of as related to activities undertaken once a work has been released. Examples of dissemination epitext include catalog records and author interviews, readings, conversations, and discussions. Useful questions for considering dissemination epitext are:

- To what kind of audience is the work targeted? Who is left out?

- What biases (if any) exist in the dissemination of the work?

- What insight do these elements provide into the author's purpose?

Reception epitext is those elements related to the evaluation of and reaction to a work. Some examples include reviews, awards, honors, and critical essays. Useful questions for considering reception epitext are:

- What do these elements tell you about the origin or purpose of the work?

- How do they influence your understanding of the work?

- How do they influence the perceived value of the work?

Extension epitext consists of elements that extend the original work in some way. Examples include sequels and prequels, parodies, pastiche, fan fiction, transmedia (adaptations), and remixes. Useful questions for considering extension epitext are:

- Do these elements help you understand the work better? Why or why not?

- How do readers/viewers of a work interact with the work?

- How do extension epitexts honor or critique the original work?

Referential epitext is elements, typically other works, that somehow connect back to the original work. Referential elements include quotations, allusions, instances of plagiarism, influences, citations, and comparisons. Useful questions for considering referential epitext are:

- What relationships exist between the works?
- Is the meaning of the original work strengthened or undermined by the work-to-work relationship?
- Is the meaning of the original work changed by the work-to-work relationship?

Finally, we might note that the first three epitextual categories—production, promotion, and dissemination—are generally within the author's and publisher's (or producer's) control, whereas the last three—reception, extension, and referential—are generally not within their control (although an obvious exception is when authors produce sequels or prequels to their own work). The functions of epitext were provided to the authors of the following chapters in order to frame our collective work.

Literacy in a Digital Age

In 2020, the National Council of Teachers of English (NCTE) released its update to the Definition of 21st Century Literacies (2008), renamed the *Definition of Literacy in a Digital Age*. NCTE shares:

> Literacy has always been a collection of communicative and sociocultural practices shared among communities. As society and technology change, so does literacy. The world demands that a literate person possess and intentionally apply a wide range of skills, competencies, and dispositions. These literacies are interconnected, dynamic, and malleable. As in the past, they are inextricably linked with histories, narratives, life possibilities, and social trajectories of all individuals and groups.

As educators and librarians, we have a responsibility to guide learners to recognize how the interconnectedness of "texts," in the broadest sense, is shaped by the histories and narratives surrounding them. Our work with peritext, and now epitext, provides an effective approach for examining the intricacies of texts and media. To be literate today, one must possess the ability to "explore and engage critically, thoughtfully, and across a wide variety of inclusive texts and tools/modalities" (NCTE, 2020), as well as recognize the multiple layers of identities, experiences, narratives, biases, and cultural experiences that may be reflected within the text proper and the texts surrounding it. The chapters in this collection do just that and provide examples of how epitextual analysis can strengthen literacy skills.

Epitext in Action

Our work in examining the applications of paratext would be incomplete without sharing a collection of work on the applications of epitext in various contexts. When considering the ever-expanding definitions of literacy, texts, and media, we wanted to share our thinking in conversation with the chapter authors. To that end, you will notice callout bubbles throughout the chapters, sharing our thinking and questioning alongside the authors' words.

These callout bubbles are a way for us to engage with the authors and with you, the reader. We hope you'll feel welcome to annotate your own thinking along the way.

Additionally, you will notice that each chapter ends with a "Reflecting on Your Learning" box. These boxes can serve as a starting point for your own learning, or perhaps frame or jump-start discussions for your professional learning community (PLC) or book clubs within your school districts, libraries, or membership organizations.

As the chapters in this book demonstrate, epitext offers a wealth of opportunities for promoting critical thinking among students at various levels. The book is organized into four main parts. Part I focuses on how epitext can be used to increase reading comprehension. Melissa Gross and Zoe Leonarczyk provide a case study of how epitext might be used to explore a young adult novel, while Sharon Kane and Deborah Heiligman discuss the use of epitext in studying biographies for children and young adults. Luke Rodesliler and Eric Federspiel explain how *MetaMaus* is a trove of epitextual elements that can offer insights into the study of Spiegelman's *Maus*. Tyler C. Sisco describes the use of fan fiction strategies to foster creativity and understanding of Steinbeck's *Of Mice and Men*.

Part II explores several ways epitext can be used to enhance critical thinking. James Blasingame examines epitext related to the prerelease, release, and reception of Anderson's *Wintergirls*. Stephanie Toliver discusses the value of reading author-created epitext, focusing on Black female speculative fiction writers. Loren Jones, Sharon L. Smith, and

Luciana C. de Oliveira describe using series books with elementary school students as a means to explore extension epitext.

Part III examines production and promotion epitext in commercials and films. Margaret Mackey considers the marketing of the 2018 film *Mary Poppins Returns* by examining various supermarket publications that were issued around the time of the film's release. Shanedra D. Nowell describes the use of book flyers and book trailers as a way of promoting media literacy through critical analysis of these advertisements. W. Kyle Jones explains how script development and storyboarding in an audio-visual production class are examples of epitext that can help students develop important media literacy skills.

Finally, Part IV focuses on epitext in digital spaces. Brady Nash discusses various kinds of video-game epitext that were incorporated into a 12th-grade English class. Jonathan M. Hollister explains how role-playing can be seen as an example of epitext in online games and how it can be used to promote a variety of literacy skills. Finally, Katie Henry and Bud Hunt describe the close connection between epitext and revision that emerged when teachers in a workshop wrote poems and then built small robots based on their poems.

Taken together, these chapters offer insight into the multifaceted phenomenon known as *epitext*. Though they have been grouped according to commonalities, they can be read in any order. The hope is that they will inspire readers to undertake their own adventures in exploring the vast, complex world of epitext.

References

Genette, G. (1997). *Paratexts: Thresholds of interpretation* (J. E. Lewin, trans.). New York: Cambridge University Press.

Gross, M., & Latham, D. (2017). The peritextual literacy framework: Using the functions of peritext to support critical thinking. *Library and Information Science Research, 39*(2): 116–23.

National Council of Teachers of English. (2020). Definition of Literacy in a Digital Age. https://ncte.org/statement/nctes-definition-literacy-digital-age

Witte, S., Latham, D., & Gross, M. (eds.) (2019). *Literacy engagement through peritextual analysis.* Chicago: American Library Association and National Council of Teachers of English.

PART I

Epitext and Comprehension

CHAPTER 1

Epitext and Young Adult Fiction

A Case Study of
Piecing Me Together

Melissa Gross and Zoe Leonarczyk

Has this happened to you? There is a new movie coming out. It sounds like it will tell an amazing story, the cast is made up of dependable actors that you like, and you're thinking this is a movie you *really* want to see. What happens next is that you're driving in your car listening to NPR or reading the Sunday *Times* and come across a review of the new movie. Your interest peaks and you pay close attention, but the review turns out to be highly critical. In that reviewer's opinion, the storyline is weak or the acting disappointing or there is some other flaw that kept the movie from fully realizing its potential. As you take in this information, you feel your interest and enthusiasm wane, and by the time the review is finished you have changed your mind and are now thinking, "I'll see something else" or "maybe I'll watch that when it's available on television."

This is one demonstration of the power of epitext. *Epitext* is a word for the wide variety of texts (and other materials) that in one way or another bring our attention to another work. Reviews, as an example, by their nature do this, as they exist mainly to talk about a book, movie, video game, website, or something else.

The authors of this chapter are a professor of information and a doctoral student who worked together teaching a course on young adult (YA) literature and then in an independent study focused on epitext. This chapter reflects their thinking as they considered the wide variety of epitext that exists around *Piecing Me Together* by Renée Watson, a work of young adult fiction, and explored some of the ways epitext related to this work can be used in the classroom (2017).

What they found was that the use of epitext in the classroom not only reveals the creative process, it can also generate creativity in students. The study of referential connections between and among works can deepen the reading experience and actively demonstrate how broad exposure to works has a cumulative effect that enlarges the sense that literature is a conversation that welcomes participation. The reading and production of extension texts, such as fan fiction, transmedia texts, and remixes, are a powerful way to engage with works and to develop a more personal relationship with reading.

The concept of epitext comes from paratext and the work of a literary theorist named Gérard Genette, who examined the elements that accompany a text, such as a table of contents, as well as things that bring our attention to a text, such as a review (1997). He calls elements that accompany a text *peritext*, and things that bring our attention to a text *epitext* (paratext = peritext + epitext) (Genette, 1997, p. 5).

Whereas peritext performs its functions by being attached to the work for which it provides a threshold, epitext is free to enjoy unlimited vistas as it travels through both physical and social spaces uttering remembrances that point to the existence of a work (Genette, 1997, p. 344). Epitext can do this because it can be fixed in virtually any type of media and can exist outside of media as well. For example, it can be as ephemeral as a comment made between people in passing. Unlike peritext, epitext can be created by anyone, not just the author, publisher, illustrator, or others involved in the production of the work. Critics, fans, teachers, interviewers, award committees, and cataloguers are all individuals who routinely create epitext, though their intent might not be paratextual (to point to the work).

Because epitext can be created by anyone, at any time, it follows that epitext can be public or private in nature. Public epitext normally assumes that the general public will be listening. Private epitext, in contrast, is generally intended for the author's own use, as with diaries or with confidences meant for a specific person or persons. Private epitext can and does often become public. Examples are the published love letters from Vladimir Nabokov to his wife Véra Slonim (2017), and the anecdotes that populate "tell-all" stories in which references that were thought to be ephemeral (like what someone said) become fixed in print. Thus, the ultimate audience epitext may reach is everyone, meaning the public at large, including both readers and nonreaders.

The reader benefits for connecting epitext to a text (and vice versa) are many. In a time when our conception of reading is changing, and in which the attainment of fluid reading skills is a concern even at the college level (Johnson, 2019), incorporating epitext into classroom teaching allows readers to explore and use various media to complement and extend their experience of a work. Incorporating media literacy and writing practices through the study of epitext may increase interest and a sense of authenticity for students by acknowledging literacy practices outside of school. For readers who are having difficulty with reading comprehension, epitext can be used to scaffold understanding by providing summaries of content, interpretations, criticisms, and appreciations others share about the work.

Epitext can be used in the classroom to demonstrate the creative process by following the trail that production of a work leaves behind. This starts with the author's process, then moves to the preproduction activities involving the author, publisher, book designer, and others involved in bringing a work to life. Genette (1997) makes the point that the production of epitext can begin before a work is even born, in forms such as correspondence, storyboards, drafts, and even diaries—all of which provide evidence of the emerging concept. This epitext exists whether or not the final project is ever actualized. Some works are started but are never born. Projects are abandoned, manuscripts are lost, and authors can die before their work is completed. However, epitext (and the production of new epitext) can have a very long life regardless of the fate of the original work. When works are born, the production of epitext can continue indefinitely past the production phase and into the promotional phase as a work is advertised, marketed, disseminated, received, and connected to other works in the great conversation that is literature increasingly extended in endless media formats. Through the study of epitext, it becomes clear that the success of a work depends on many things and people and takes place over time. Epitext, in calling out works, can have many types of influence on readers, nonreaders, and society.

Epitext Types

Some general ways that epitext can be useful in a classroom or library context include:

1. Scaffolding comprehension of the text. Seeing what various kinds of epitext have to say about what is being read informs readers about meaning.

2. Incorporating media that is attractive to students into class discussion. Epitext occurs in all kinds of media and forms, allowing for the use of social media, transmedia, fan fiction, and other sources students may be familiar with and find interesting.

3. Demonstrating the creative process. As shown in this chapter, epitext can highlight the life cycle of a work, revealing the author's process and intentions behind a work as well as how a work changes as it goes through the production process.

> Consider "fractured fairy-tales" as an example of this. How does knowledge of an original folktale inform the reading of the same tale in a fractured version? Does not knowing the original story limit the enjoyment of the fractured tale?

4. Encouraging creativity in finding gaps in works that the reader can fill in. When gaps in a work are revealed, these gaps can become an opportunity for discussion as well as an opportunity for readers to fill those gaps through their own creativity, as in fan fiction.

5. Experiencing how broad exposure to works deepens the reading experience. Supplementing knowledge of a work with exposure to how others understand, evaluate, use, or think about the work increases understanding of intertextuality and personal experience of a work.

6. Recognizing that the success of a text depends on many players. Epitext reveals the array of people and texts that can affect how broadly knowledge that a work exists and its quality is transmitted to the general public.

7. Understanding the potential effects of pointing to a text. Readers can not only see the effects of different types of epitext, but can exercise their own sphere of influence by disseminating their own ideas about, assessments of, and reactions to a work.

8. Enhancing the reading experience. Perceptions of reading can move away from an isolated individual experience and move toward an awareness that texts and reading are part of a great conversation that is continuous and rich.

As discussed in the introduction to this volume, Witte, Latham, and Gross, in working with Genette's theory of paratext, recognized that the functions of epitext can be categorized into six types: production, promotion, dissemination, reception, extension, and referential. These types provide a frame for the discussion that follows here. Each of the six functions of epitext is discussed, including general examples of epitext that serve these functions as well. We also present specific instances of epitext that point to *Piecing Me Together,* and ideas for incorporating epitext into the study of a work are offered to help illustrate how teachers and librarians can use epitext in educational contexts. It should be remembered that it is possible for epitext to serve more than one function. Thus, the functions of epitext can be seen as a lens, rather than a strict typology in which the various forms epitext take would be expected to fall into mutually exclusive categories.

Piecing Me Together

Piecing Me Together is both a Newbery Honor book and a Coretta Scott King Author Award winner. It tells the story of Jade, who is traversing two worlds: the all-White, upper-class high school she attends as a scholarship student and her predominantly African American, economically disadvantaged home neighborhood. Jade is an artist and intent on success, and she is also aware of how different aspects of herself (such as gender, race, and social status) affect how people see and react to her, shattering her into parts when she wants to be whole. This recognition that a person can experience multiple sources of discrimination based on the various identities they hold is called *intersectionality*, a term coined by Kimberlé Crenshaw (1989).

> A great exercise for understanding identity through intersectionality can be found at https://www.youtube.com/watch?v=71UMDBNCTJI

One of her goals in high school is to take part in a study-abroad program where she can fine-tune her Spanish-language skills. Instead, she is offered the opportunity to participate in a mentoring program called Woman to Woman: A Mentorship Program for African American Girls.

Unfortunately, her assigned mentor, Maxine, is more interested in her own life and problems than she is in having an authentic relationship with Jade. Everywhere Jade looks, she sees how her race, gender, and economic status affect how people see and treat her. Her exploration of her identity as she navigates relationships with her family, peers, teachers, her mentor, and the world at large make for a nuanced and revealing narrative on the intersectionality of being. Jade's experience of the world will mirror the experiences of many readers who are not often depicted in young adult fiction and provide a basis for potentially rich, in-depth discussions that can lead to increased awareness of how people are marginalized, what that feels like, and a better understanding of how identity shapes experience. A study of some of the epitext that exists around this novel can be used to further explicate its themes, consider the quality of the work, and assess how readers might come to know about it and what influence epitext might have on the reading experience.

Production Epitext

Production epitext relates to the pre-, during-, and post-production stages of a work. Examples of production epitext include author correspondence, drafts, outlines, storyboards, author journals/diaries, and page proofs. One of the most accessible examples of production epitext for librarians and educators is the advance reader's copy or advance review copy (ARC). ARCs are uncorrected proofs of books that circulate before publication. They are sent to reviewers and other influencers for feedback, and also are often given away at professional association meeting exhibit halls, such as at the American Library Association conferences. ARCs are meant to generate early reviews and buzz around the book, but because they are not the final official version of the work, they capture an interim stage in the production process. Because they are pre-publication texts, they may not include the final cover art, may contain typos and other mistakes, and may differ from the final version of the work if other changes are made in response to feedback from advance readers.

The study of early drafts of works has a long history in literary studies. A very recent example of interest in early versions was recently written up in the *New York Times* (Christensen, 2019) on the publication of Virginia Woolf's original manuscript for *Mrs. Dalloway*. Now readers familiar with the story can see how what she set out to do changed between the production of this manuscript and the final published version.

Production Epitext for Piecing Me Together

Prior to the formal publication of *Piecing Me Together*, advance reader's copies circulated among reviewers, bloggers, and others who have reviewer relationships with the publisher or who requested a copy through online sites such as NetGalley (https://www.netgalley.com/). Once people received and read the *Piecing Me Together* ARC, reviews were posted on blogs, Goodreads, and major retail sites. Introducing students to ARCs and helping them discover how they are different from the final published work can provide a glimpse into the kinds of changes that result from the production process. A discussion focused on why the text and/or illustrations might have changed can lead to thinking more deeply about the creative process and how that can be influenced by epitext that is generated before a work is published.

Production Epitext in the Classroom

When discussing the production function in a classroom, advance reader copies can be used to compare the differences before official publication and after publication. Differences in appearance, major noticeable changes in the text, and the setup of the book can be discussed. Reading early reviews in addition to the work itself can stimulate a lively discussion of what opinions or reactions might have influenced the author's story or strengthened the author's commitment to telling their story in a certain way. When looking at examples of the promotional epitext, ask students to consider these questions:

- What does production epitext tell you about how the work?

- What do these epitexts tell you about how the work was developed?

- What do they tell you about the sources used or the inspiration behind the creation of the work?

- Were there events or junctures where the work found its life or lost its way?

Promotion Epitext

The function of promotion epitext is to generate interest in a work in order to increase readership or sales. Some promotional epitext is the result of marketing and advertising activities. Others generate publicity in more subtle ways, but all promotional epitext serves to raise awareness of a work. Examples of promotional epitext include, but are not limited to, TV and video commercials, print advertisements, posters, flyers, book trailers, bookmarks, book bags, paraphernalia, video previews, author websites, and author social media. Book and movie release events, as well as premieres for these and other media, are also promotional in nature. Appropriate promotion of a work recognizes that the success of a work depends on many players and circumstances. Diverse promotion texts allow awareness of a work to be raised among a wider population and can lead to greater access to a work. Promotion texts are produced by many people or entities, including the author, the publisher, book retail companies, and others.

> Students might critique the design of an author's website and discuss how effectively (or not) it promotes a particular work or works.

Promotional Epitext for Piecing Me Together

Renée Watson's author website is an example of epitext that points to her book, *Piecing Me Together*. Her home page displays large graphics of her works and provides links to retrospective pages on the texts (http://www.reneewatson.net/). *Piecing Me Together* is the second graphic displayed and features the original book jacket with the protagonist, Jade, front and center on the cover, along with the badges from the Newbery Honor and Coretta Scott King awards this book received. Clicking on this graphic leads to an interview podcast with Renée Watson discussing *Piecing Me Together*. Meanwhile, clicking on the "BOOKS" tab of the website takes the user to a page dedicated to Watson's publications. Of Watson's works, *Piecing Me Together* is one of the two books highlighted on this page. The page features blurbs authors have written in response to reading the book as well as links to texts and interviews on the book. Clicking on this page's graphic of the cover of *Piecing Me Together* takes the user to the Barnes and Noble page where the book can be purchased. The texts and links on this page promote the book and work toward convincing people to purchase and read the book.

Another example of promotional epitext is author participation on social media sites. These handles help authors to personally promote their works and bridge a gap between authors and readers. Renée Watson's Instagram page (@harlemportland) is a space for Watson to connect with readers and promote her current works and events. The graphics relating to *Piecing Me Together* share information and advertisements pertaining to current events and information on the book.

Watson's Twitter page (@reneewauthor) is very similar to her Instagram page, but with a more textual approach. Through these social media sites, it is easy to find out where Watson will be and what events she is participating in at these locations, as well as to learn more about her works and find interviews in which she has discussed her personal creative process. These promotional texts can assist potential readers in shaping their views on the work as well as connecting with the author and her own point of view on her works.

Promotional Epitext in the Classroom

The author's website and social media sites can be compared in the classroom when discussing promotional epitext. Students can view the different forms that the promotion of a text may take and talk about the level of effectiveness of these epitexts in terms of generating new readership or increasing sales. Some questions for discussion include:

- What does promotional epitext tell you about the work?

- What audiences are various promotional epitexts trying to reach?

- How might these epitexts affect the reader's view of the work?

- What makes promotional epitext successful in generating interest in a work?

Dissemination Epitext

The dissemination function of epitext describes the ways in which a work and knowledge of the content of a work are shared, often with the outcome of making knowledge of a work more public. Dissemination epitext differs from promotional epitext in that the primary objective of dissemination is the sharing of content, not the marketing and advertising of a work, although such epitext may also enlarge readership or increase sales. Dissemination epitext differs from reception epitext in that it is not primarily engaged in examining works critically. Examples of dissemination epitext are author readings, interviews, and lectures. Author readings and lectures take place both formally and informally and are common bookstore events, as are gatherings in an academic context. Though it is often possible to buy books at these events, the author is the main draw, as is the chance to experience the work firsthand in the author's own voice. These events are often ephemeral, in that you have to be there to have the experience, although it is becoming increasingly common for hosts to video- or audio-record readings in order to make them available outside the event. Similarly, interviews with authors increase awareness of works, but the author is generally the primary draw.

It is also possible for author readings and other dissemination epitext to serve a promotional function. In discussing the functions of epitext, students can consider the various functions that an example of epitext might serve and how to assign functions to epitext.

Dissemination Epitext for Piecing Me Together

On Saturday, January 5, at 6:30 p.m., Renée Watson read aloud and discussed writing for young people at Lesley University ("Renee Watson Headlines," 2018). It does not appear that this lecture was captured for later access, highlighting the ephemeral nature of some dissemination epitext. A second example is an interview with the author for NPR (Watson, 2018). In this example, the entire radio interview is not reproduced for the reader. Instead, portions of the interview transcript are presented on the NPR website. Two other short interviews that provide transcripts, but not voice recordings, available on the Web include an interview by Jenn Strattman (n.d.) and the Children's and Young Adult's Bloggers' Literary Awards interview with Renée Watson (n.d.).

Dissemination Epitext in the Classroom

Short interviews, such as those just described, can be used in the classroom or library to explore what readers or potential readers like to see when they engage with this kind of epitext. Students can compose interview questions and engage in role-playing where one student takes the author's role and the other performs the interview.

Questions to address include:

- Is there any potential bias in the way dissemination epitexts are distributed? Consider who the presumed audience is, and the type of media used to speak to the presumed audience.

- When interviews are not provided in full, what content may be missing? Why might some content have been deleted?

- Does dissemination epitext reveal anything about the author's purpose?

Reception Epitext

Reception epitext expresses reactions to and critical evaluations of a work. Examples of this function include reviews and critical essays, awards and honors, and social media sharing. Texts that fall in the reception category stem from people other than the author writing about the original work. The reception function shares these opinions and feelings and can help encourage people to read the work or to forgo it. Both good reviews and bad reviews have the power to affect readers' decision to engage with a work. So, in some ways, reception epitext are related to promotional epitext in that they can stimulate interest and make knowledge of a work more public; however, promotional epitext's primary function is not critical in nature, whereas reception epitext's is.

The Internet has provided a platform that can easily disseminate the reception a work is receiving, allowing these reactions to reach a wide range of people. Social media has become a large part of society and remains a major influence. Most people are familiar with common social media sites, such as Twitter and Instagram, in which hashtags can be used as a form of searching for books.

Reception Epitext for Piecing Me Together

Searching the hashtag #piecingmetogether on Instagram and Twitter pulls up many posts made regarding the book. These posts share tidbits of thoughts and feelings regarding the book. The Instagram posts add the element of pictures and allow users to write longer captions. These posts often have reviews that share the user's reception of the book and allow others to add their thoughts. The Twitter posts are capped at 280 characters and are often short snippets on the work instead of extensive reviews.

Reception Epitext in the Classroom

Incorporating the social media aspect of reception into a discussion of the book *Piecing Me Together* can allow a connection to be made with students who have grown up surrounded by social media sites. After discussing the reception function in a classroom, students can complete an activity in which they compose either a tweet or an Instagram post based on the book. Students will then have a chance to put the reception function into action and determine how their "posts" could influence the success of a book. There are a number of questions that can generate discussion when viewing examples of reception epitext. Students can consider:

- How does reception epitext influence how we understand or respond to a work?

- Has reception epitext has ever motivated them to engage, or not to engage, with a work?

- Has reception epitext ever changed their mind about a work?

- What do we learn about a work from engaging with reception texts?

Extension Epitext

Extension epitext takes an original work as a starting point. The types of extension epitexts that are possible vary widely. Authors may choose to extend their own works by producing sequels or prequels to the original story. Extension epitext can also be produced by people other than the author. One form these texts can take is an imitation of the original, as in pastiche, parody, fan fiction, transmedia, and remixes. Another form of extension epitext is discussion or teaching guides developed to promote or facilitate discussion about a work or to assist in teaching about a work. There are a number of producers of these texts, including the author and the publisher as well as teachers, librarians, and book clubs.

Extension Epitext for Piecing Me Together

"Piecing Me Together: A Discussion Guide about Race, Class, and Intersectionality," produced for Bloomsbury (Cappy & O'Brien, n.d.), is an excellent example of a resource meant to facilitate the use of work in a classroom, library, or another learning context. It assists the discussion leader by explaining important concepts that can be explored in thinking about the book, providing examples from the work, providing citations to resources outside the work, suggesting classroom activities and discussion questions, and providing information about the author. This type of extension text can be used wholesale or as a starting point for lesson plan development. It can also be used by individual readers to extend or deepen their understanding of the book.

Extension Epitext in the Classroom

With any extension epitext, questions to explore are:

- What kind of relationship do the producers and readers of extension epitexts have with the original work?

- What effect does the extension epitext have on readers' experience of the original work?

- Does familiarity with the original work matter when reading an extension epitext?

Referential Epitext

Referential epitext describes the various kinds of relationships that can exist between and among works. Sometimes these relationships are very close, as in the use of direct quotes, citations, or work copied without attribution (plagiarism). However, referential relationships can run the gamut from very direct and obvious links to relationships that are slight and perhaps only apparent to those "in the know." Examples include indirect references such as allusion

> Students can discuss the ethical use of information by considering satire and pastiche and how far away from an original a writer must be from the original to avoid plagiarism.

or the influence of one writer's work on another. The referential function is a good example of what Genette meant in pointing out that epitext has no precise limits because it "gradually disappears into, among other things, the totality of the authorial discourse" (Genette, 1997, p. 356).

Referential Epitext for Piecing Me Together

One example of a referential connection is the use of a work as a point of comparison to another work. An instance of this occurs in a conversation published in the *English Journal* about the book *The Hate U Give* by Angie Thomas (Ebarvia, Parker, & Schmidt, 2018). The purpose of the conversation was to share how a work considered part of the literature of resistance can be used with students in the classroom and the power of including such works in class reading. *Piecing Me Together* is mentioned as an example of a related title that students who read and liked *The Hate U Give* would also be interested in reading, and a photograph of the book jacket is reproduced on the page.

Referential Epitext in the Classroom

As the column about *The Hate U Give* is brief, it could easily be used in the classroom or library to generate discussion about referential relationships between works and what effect, if any, they have on readers. Once students are oriented to the referential function of epitext, it can become a topic for any classroom reading. Students can consider the reasons why authors point to other works in telling their own story or in sharing information. They can begin to notice when a new story has epitext of another tale, even if that tale is not directly identified by the author, and reflect on how and why that happens in literature.

Students can consider:

- Is it important to have firsthand knowledge of a work that is mentioned or suggested in another work?
- Does firsthand knowledge deepen or change the reader's experience?
- Does ignorance of the title referred to limit understanding of the work?
- Does referential epitext motivate readers to track down and potentially read referenced works?

Conclusion

There is an almost unlimited array of epitext available related to works of interest in classroom and library contexts. Understanding the types of epitext that exist allows for the discussion of works to consider the production process as well as the various players involved in promoting and disseminating works. The life cycle of a work is more fully revealed as a work's reception is considered as well as the degree to which it is extended, re-envisioned, used, and even stolen by others. Epitext reveals the wide variety of responses individuals have to a text and provides an opportunity for readers to take other points of view into account and to reconsider their own relationship to a work.

The uses of epitext in the classroom or library are many. Epitext can broaden and deepen an individual's reading experience. It can increase understanding of a work, and encourage personal creativity in response to a work. Epitext reveals the wide array of ways that exist to point back to a text and influence its reception. Students who are exposed to Genette's concepts may find themselves identifying epitext on their own as they consume various media and experience the vast number of relationships a work can have with the texts that point back to it. They will also develop an awareness that this is a conversation they can be part of: not only in the classroom, but also in their personal relationship with media.

Reflecting on Your Learning

What role has epitext played in your own development as a reader? Has epitext ever changed your mind about a book, movie, or other work? What effect did it have on your opinion of the work or your decision to read, view, or otherwise experience the work?

References

Cappy, K., & O'Brien, A. S. (n.d.). *Piecing Me Together: A discussion guide about race, class, gender, and intersectionality.* https://media.bloomsbury.com/rep/files/Piecing%20Me%20Together%20Guide.pdf

Children's and Young Adult's Bloggers' Literary Awards. (2018, May 1). *Interview with Renée Watson.* https://www.cybils.com/2018/05/interview-with-renee-watson.html

Christensen, L. (2019, June 14). A glimpse of Virginia Woolf's original manuscript for "Mrs. Dalloway." *New York Times.* https://www.nytimes.com/2019/06/14/books/review/virginia-woolf-mrs-dalloway.html?ref=headline&nl_art=&te=1&nl=book-review&emc=edit_bk_20190614?campaign_id=69&instance_id=10229&segment_id=14319&user_id=d145064706ee9244f5f749e4889121af&regi_id=62813372edit_bk_20190614

Crenshaw, K. (1989). Demarginalizing the intersection of race and sex: A Black feminist critique of antidiscrimination doctrine, feminist theory and antiracist politics. *University of Chicago Legal Forum*, 1989 (1, Article 8). http://chicagounbound.uchicago.edu/uclf/vol1989/iss1/8

Ebarvia, T., Parker, K., & Schmidt, P. S. (2018). #BlackLivesMatter: When real life and YA fiction converge. *English Journal*, *107*(5): 92–95.

Genette, G. (1997). *Paratexts: Thresholds of interpretation* (J. E. Lewin, trans.). Cambridge, UK: Cambridge University Press.

Johnson, S. (2019, April 26). The fall, and rise, of reading. *Chronicle of Higher Education*, *65*(31). https://www.chronicle.com/article/the-fall-and-rise-of-reading

Nabokov, V. (2017). *Letters to Véra*. New York: Vintage Books.

Renée Watson headlines winter evening reading series. (2018, December 18). Lesley University. https://lesley.edu/news/renee-watson-headlines-winter-evening-reading-series

Strattman, J. (n.d.). *Interview with Renée Watson*. Pine Manor College. http://www.pmc.edu/interview-with-renee-watson

Watson, R. (2017). *Piecing Me Together*. New York: Bloomsbury.

Watson, R. (2018, February 17). *"Piecing Me Together" Novelist says she writes to help kids feel seen* [interview]. National Public Radio. https://www.npr.org/2018/02/17/586479140/piecing-me-together-novelist-says-she-writes-to-help-kids-feel-seen

CHAPTER 2

Epitextual Analysis of Biographies
Enhancing Disciplinary Literacy

Sharon Kane with Deborah Heiligman

Introduction

Brilliance. Passion. Quirkiness. These are traits found in many subjects of biographies. Sometimes they are also traits that can be identified in the biographers who choose to write about particular brilliant, passionate, and quirky individuals. Deborah Heiligman, well-known for award-winning biographies written for children and teens, might meet these criteria (though she will get a chance at the end of this chapter to deny any quirks). How will readers of biographies written by Heiligman be affected when encouraged to explore epitextual materials related to the texts and their author? This is one thing I set out to discover while teaching three different classes during a recent semester.

Statement of Issues to Be Considered

Louise Rosenblatt, herself a brilliant, passionate, and extraordinary scholar, gave us a lens through which to examine readers' responses to texts. What they bring to a text is hugely important, as is their purpose for reading the text. In recent years, scholars have demonstrated that reading, writing, and responding can look very different depending on one's field of study. This chapter brings together aspects of Rosenblatt's transactional theory with aspects of disciplinary literacy, and considers how teachers might enhance readers' experience with biographies by exploring their epitextual elements. It describes three groups' interactions with biographies written by Deborah Heiligman, and several types of epitext (some found, some created) related to those biographies.

How the Work Is Situated in Epitext

This chapter concentrates on two of the functional types of epitext discussed in the introduction to this volume: reception and extension. Students in three classes were given opportunities to freely respond to at least one Heiligman biography, then explore any examples of the work's epitext they found interesting. Some read reviews or award acceptance speeches, and responded to those in addition to the biographies themselves. (They were struck by the line "I want to thank Vincent and Theo" in one award acceptance speech [Heiligman, 2018]). Many went on to create their own art and/or written texts, using multiple formats and types of media as they forged new connections, expressed emotions, and honored or critiqued the biographies and their subjects. By doing so, they added to the beauty and wonder of our learning communities. One class worked in anticipation of a scheduled videoconference with Deborah Heiligman.

Review of the Relevant Literature

Transactional Theory

Louise Rosenblatt spent several decades developing, refining, exploring, and promoting transactional theory. She uses the term *poem* in a unique way, to signify what occurs when a specific reader comes together with a specific text at a particular time and place. The relation between the reader and the text is not linear, and neither is prioritized over the other. The prior knowledge, experiences, and attitudes the reader brings to the text are crucial, as is the reader's purpose.

According to Rosenblatt (1978), if readers' primary concern is what they will take away from the reading—that is, information, facts, directions—that is *efferent* reading. If their main purpose relates to what they are living through during the reading event—paying attention to attitudes, feelings, and associations that have been evoked by the text—that is *aesthetic* reading. A text can be read efferently or aesthetically, and readers can shift back and forth between these stances.

We might pause here to ask how we, or our students, would be likely to read biographies such as the ones by Heiligman that are discussed in this chapter. If they had self-selected one or more biographies and were reading them by choice, chances are their main purpose would be aesthetic, though they would certainly be learning information about the biographical subjects and their work. However, Rosenblatt worries that some readers do not learn to make the shift from the efferent toward the aesthetic end of the spectrum. "[M]ultiple and equally valid possibilities are often inherent in the same text

> To what extent is nonfiction especially susceptible to an almost exclusive emphasis on efferent reading? What is lost when little, if any, attention is given to the aesthetic stance when teaching/reading nonfiction?

in its transactions with different readers under different conditions" (Rosenblatt, 1978, p. 75). However, "[i]n our schools, the emphasis in the teaching of reading is almost entirely on the efferent stance. Comprehension in reading tests is assumed mainly to be of this type" (p. 79). Would we agree that this is still a valid concern today? How might we guide students to appreciate reading from a more aesthetic stance?

Disciplinary Literacy

A disciplinary literacy framework recognizes that reading, writing, and thinking happen differently in distinct academic fields. Stances and styles of scientific papers differ from those composed by historians, musicians, psychologists, educators, mathematicians, and poets. Practitioners read differently, and they create and share knowledge in specific ways. A position statement by the International Literacy Association, titled *Collaborating for Success: The Vital Role of Content Teachers in Developing Disciplinary Literacy with Students in Grades 6–12* (2015) emphasizes the specialized skill sets and unique literacy demands of the disciplines. Our role as teachers in secondary school subjects is to welcome students as apprentices in our fields. Wide and varied reading is a means to accomplish this goal; thus, biographies are perfect texts to introduce students to key figures, not just in terms of accomplishments, but as real people with flaws, passions, eccentricities, curiosity, disabilities, setbacks, literacy habits, and complicated relationships, just like them!

In addition, biographies have the capacity to show readers that practitioners read, write, view, and think in ways particular to their discourse communities. The featured biographical subjects—Charles Darwin, Vincent van Gogh, and Paul Erdős—followed the disciplinary rules of their fields, or consciously chose to break them. All three read a lot and wrote and created prolifically. They were in constant correspondence with colleagues. Heiligman presents her subjects through their relationships, while showing them at work in discipline-specific ways. Her books provide peritext, such as book covers and author's notes, consistent with rules of *her* discipline of nonfiction writing, thus allowing curious readers a rich experience. Disciplinary literacy at its best!

Context

In a graduate course titled "Literature, Art, and Media," students were assigned to read Deborah Heiligman's *Vincent and Theo: The Van Gogh Brothers* (2017) and to respond freely in words and/or images. The next week, after a brief introduction to the functions of epitext, they were given free rein to explore resources related to the text, the biography's subjects, or the author; and/or to extend the text through transmedia or writing of their own. Teachers themselves, they reveled in the freedom of this intellectual and artistic challenge. The following week, we read *The Boy Who Loved Math: The Improbable Life of Paul Erdős* (2013) in class, and again they pursued various paths leading to epitextual study of that work.

In an undergraduate course, "Literacy in the Content Areas," some students selected Heiligman's *Charles and Emma: The Darwins' Leap of Faith* (2009) to respond to and then discuss in a literature circle. We read *The Boy Who Loved Math* together, and began looking for resources, reviews, and other examples of epitext. They pursued the search and created extensions outside of class.

In an alternative high school setting, I read aloud *The Boy Who Loved Math* and invited students to respond in writing as well as orally. Later, we made connections to other texts, including additional biographical treatments of the mathematician Paul Erdős, Deborah Heiligman's webpage, and the novel *The Curious Incident of the Dog in the Night-time* (Haddon, 2003), whose narrator loves prime numbers arguably as much as Paul Erdős did. We perused *G Is for Googol: A Math Alphabet Book* (Schwartz, 1998) and then made mathematical predictions as we experimented with making Möbius strips to help us comprehend the concept of infinity. Over the next week, students wrote questions in preparation for the scheduled videoconference with Deborah Heiligman (all student names appearing here are pseudonyms).

Practical Methods/Application of Approach

Rosenblatt's transactional theory was evident in readers' responses to Heiligman's biographies. Individuals picked up on different details; appreciated different aspects of the subjects' struggles, accomplishments, and relationships; and chose to represent their interpretations and affective reactions to the texts using a wide variety of styles, formats, and tools, resulting in sharing sessions that illuminated new paths for their classmates. Our collection of materials included:

- Allison's color-coded timeline ("number line") of Paul Erdős's life events using only prime numbers;

- Graphic organizers and collages containing images and text, such as "body biographies" of Vincent and Theo Van Gogh, drawn and colored by Robin;

- David's image of Paul Erdős's face filled with prime numbers, created using Photoshop;

- Lists of prefixes and suffixes, as well as solutions to puzzles, that illustrator LeUyen Pham incorporated into the pages of *The Boy Who Loved Math.*

Transmedia was evident in Amelia's creation, which used large letters, each cut out from a copy of one of Van Gogh's paintings, spelling VINCENT, superimposed on the text of lyrics from Don McLean's "Vincent" (1972).

We assembled a huge folder of resources, including a packet of fascinating obituaries published after the death of Paul Erdős at the age of 83, while he attended a lecture at a math conference. These could lead to a study of the obituary genre. One review of Paul Hoffman's biography *The Man Who Loved Only Numbers: The Story of Paul Erdős and the Search for Mathematical Truth* (1998) is titled "Planning an Infinite Stay" (Alexander, 1998), playing on the facts that Erdős was fascinated with the concept of infinity (as are Deborah Heiligman and now many of the high school students); and that he had no permanent address, but rather traveled around the world, living out of a suitcase and relying on the hospitality of other mathematicians who were willing to collaborate when he knocked on their doors and announced, "'My brain is open'" (Heiligman, 2013, p. 24).

Both Paul Erdős and Deborah Heiligman might be happy to know that our classes became more playful as our study continued. One graduate student, Allison, brought in a game using a "Hundreds Chart" she used with her first-graders after reading *The Boy Who Loved Math* to them, and we paired off and played with intensity. During the time of this project, a momentous event occurred in the mathematical community: Karen Uhlenbeck was awarded the 2019 Abel Prize for her work in the area of geometric analysis, becoming the first woman to receive the honor (as well as the equivalent of about $700,000). We celebrated like she was one of us; because of our investigation into Paul Erdős's life and work, we were part of her discourse community, and we were passionate.

In *A Literature of Questions: Nonfiction for the Critical Child* (2018), Sanders discusses the importance of equivocation in nonfiction for encouraging young people to engage with the information.

It was especially noticeable in the graduate students' responses and those of the teachers and staff of the alternative high school that the disciplinary fields they belonged to played a part in how they transacted with the texts, as well as with related epitext. Bradley, an art teacher, discussed his lifelong fascination with van Gogh and connected his knowledge with the new things he learned as well as his attention to *how* Deborah Heiligman treated areas about which scholars do not necessarily concur:

> What I was unaware of was how many times he ventured into careers beyond the arts. His time as a teacher and into religious work with the poor highlight the side of Vincent that truly valued all life and wanted to selflessly give. . . . The incident of his death was also of great debate over the years and I'm glad the author chose to at least mention its possibility. Knowing how selfless Vincent was throughout his life lends itself even more to these theories that what was believed to have happened may have been more Vincent covering up for others' inflictions and accidents.

Amelia, a graduate student and aspiring history teacher, contributed a response to her exploration of epitext related to *Vincent and Theo* that primarily talked about the research she had done for her undergraduate honors thesis on Frederick Law Olmstead, the architect of Central Park. She talked animatedly about how fascinating she found Deborah Heiligman's explanations of her research in several acceptance speeches related to awards given to *Vincent and Theo*, as well as on her website. Amelia's own passion for research became increasingly evident as she stayed after class, telling me more about the subject of *her* work of biography. I pulled Marilyn Nelson's *My Seneca Village* (2015) from my office shelves, explaining that though I knew nothing of Frederick Law Olmstead, I had learned about the displacement of people in order to make way for Central Park in this historical verse novel, also thoroughly researched. Amelia took it home, and the next week came in with a found poem using text from *My Seneca Village*. Our class, realizing that one connection was leading to more connections, which led to new creations that stimulated yet more connections, wondered how far out the concept of epitext could go. Was the epitext of any text potentially infinite? Students reminded each other of a novel we had read earlier, Susin Nielsen's *We Are All Made of Molecules* (2015); and recalled the projects and performances we had participated in to celebrate International Dot Day, also having themes of connection.

Transmedia responses and disciplinary differences were also demonstrated during our conversation with Deborah. When I entered the high school classroom on the day of the videoconference, students were sitting on the floor, with their multicolored Möbius strips having clearly multiplied and morphed since I had last been there. Some had been decorated; some were being worn as bracelets; many were played with throughout the session. One student stood up to ask her question draped in them, explaining that she just could not stop making them ever since she had learned how. Deborah nodded affirmatively, saying that one of her sons had gone through a Möbius strip phase. Brooks, the social studies teacher, was thrilled to tell the group that he had just seen the newly released movie *Avengers: Endgame*, and part of the mystery involved Möbius strips, and he had understood because of our exploration of mathematical principles the previous week. Connections indeed!

Sarah, a teaching assistant and aspiring English teacher, told Deborah she is writing a children's book about chaos theory, and asked for advice. Deborah suggested focusing on a person, as she had by showing readers that Paul Erdős, while quirky, still found a way to be in the world, at which point Sarah nodded, saying softly, "Bernoulli." Deborah talked of her present process of working on a biography of geneticist Barbara McClintock, tentatively titled *The Girl Who Loved Science*. She also discussed how she had come to write *Torpedoed: The True Story of the World War II Sinking of "The Children's Ship"* (2019), which was in press at the time of our conference. She showed photographs of people and

> Some kinds of epitext are quite ephemeral while others are more permanent. By the same token, some kinds of epitext are public while others are private. What are the implications of this for engaging in epitextual analysis?

artifacts as she described her interviews and research adventures. She had taken on the role of teacher, and was simultaneously adding to the epitext of her works.

One student was more interested in Deborah's own life than in those featured in her books. He asked her whether, if she could start over, as an author or in her life, she would do anything differently. Deborah pondered the question, then gave an answer that caused the group to pause. "I guess I'd spend less time comparing myself to others. I'd worry less, and be happy with myself. I look at pictures of my young self. I thought I was too fat, too dorky. I wish I could have liked this cute girl more."

Additional Applications

After the videoconference, I wrote to Deborah, asking if she had ever played around with bringing her biographical subjects together in her mind. She replied:

> I love the idea of my people talking to each other. I would love to think of Charles Darwin at the same table as Vincent van Gogh. WHAT WOULD HAPPEN? They were both geniuses, but two less likely friends . . . yet, somehow I think Charles would bring out the best in Vincent. I think Paul and Vincent would hit it off. Would Emma and Vincent? I think so. What about Theo, who would Theo get on with? Probably all of them, in his own way . . .

Students can go anywhere once they are introduced to the idea of biographical time travel, a type of fanfiction (Kane, 2020). Paul Erdős was a great collaborator. Choose notable people in several disciplines, and imagine how they would respond to Paul's famous greeting, "My brain is open." Here's an example:

Paul Erdős: (pointing to Charles Darwin's children). You have wonderful epsilons. Would you like to collaborate and publish something together? That would mean you'd have an Erdős Number of 1!

Charles Darwin: Oh, I generally sit on my data for a couple of decades before publishing. I don't think we work at the same pace.

You could bring other mathematicians and scientists to the table. Allow Fibonacci, August Möbius, Sophie Germain, and Ada Lovelace to participate with Erdős in a symposium session on patterns and infinity. It would be fascinating to bring Charles and Emma Darwin to a present-day conference on genetics, where Francis Collins could tell them about heading the Human Genome Project, and talk about how religious belief and the theory of evolution are not mutually exclusive or incompatible. Darwin would get along with passionate animal scientist Sy Montgomery, author of *The Soul of an Octopus* (2015) and *How to Be a Good Creature: A Memoir in Thirteen Animals* (2018), among many others. And while he is here, maybe he could give a lecture in a school in a state where teachers are limited in what they can teach on the topic of evolution. Let us invite Barbara McClintock to this conference as well.

A variation of the biography time-travel assignment allows students to bring fictional characters together with the biographical subjects in Heiligman's texts. Christopher Boone, narrator of *The Curious Incident of the Dog in the Night-time* (Haddon, 2003), and Early Auden, the title character in Clare Vanderpool's *Navigating Early* (2013), are both obsessively interested in math concepts, either prime numbers or pi, and would therefore love to meet Paul Erdős. All three share similar quirks (at least as perceived by the neurotypical people in their lives) and uneven profiles in terms of talents and (dis)abilities, as well as a sense of adventure and willingness to sacrifice much during their quests for knowledge. All learn to negotiate their worlds, deal with others, and empower themselves. Suzy, the main character of *The Thing about Jellyfish*, by Ali Benjamin (2015), is a passionate researcher who would find kindred spirits in Darwin and Sy Montgomery. And Klee Alden, the grieving protagonist of Gae Polisner's *In Sight of Stars* (2018) might understand mental illness, art, and life in new ways if he could meet Vincent van Gogh, who was his late father's hero as well as his own.

> Such time-travel assignments could involve students' producing prose narratives, play-scripts, poems, and even drawings.

Conclusion

After any lesson or unit, we teachers want to know if students have been changed as a result of the learning process. Although I did not conduct a formal study, student comments led me to believe that exploring the epitext related to literature can be enriching. Amelia, after listening to Deborah's speech addressed to the Society of Children's Book Writers and Illustrators, wrote in her journal "She *knows* Vincent." In class Amelia quoted Deborah's closing lines of the speech, and said, "It made me like the book that much more." During another class, when we happened to be celebrating Beverly Cleary's 103rd birthday, Mustafa quietly noted, "By the way, 103 is a prime number."

Where does epitext end if we keep connecting the dots of our responses, and spreading our enthusiasm to others? I shared with my students a one-line email I received from my college roommate after a recent visit, during which I had (of course) shown her the book *Literacy Engagement through Peritextual Analysis* (Witte, Latham, & Gross, 2019) and told her about my chapter in progress for this book. "Don't you find it odd that a book's *epilogue* is part of its *peritext*?" Ellen's email asked. Students thought for a moment, laughed, and then started listing other words containing the prefixes "peri-" and "epi-". Do our lists become part of the epitext of those two scholarly works?

It is beginning to look like we are epitextually navigating vast, expansive spaces, reaching toward infinity, which Deborah Heiligman and Paul Erdős would applaud.

Response by Deborah Heiligman to This Chapter

I loved reading this chapter. You can't imagine how gratifying it is for an author to see her work spiraling out beyond the text into people's lives and interests and further reading. I absolutely adore the idea of readers taking the people I've written about and extending their relationships with them, either separately or together. I laughed aloud at the conversation between Paul Erdős and Charles Darwin, especially when Darwin says, "Oh, I generally sit on my data for a couple of decades before publishing." I think my Barbara McClintock book will take as long to be published as *The Origin of Species*. Though I am definitely not comparing my mind to Darwin's!

When I write a book I have a kind of dual mindset going. One is to forget about the audience, and just write the book that I want to write. The other is to very much think about the audience and aim to get everything about the book right for those readers. I juggle those from day to day, week to week, sometimes hour to hour. Now, after reading this, I wonder if I will also think about how readers can take what I write further into their lives and intellectual exploration. And I wonder if that will affect how I write a book. I will have to get back to you about that!

On a personal note, I was rather shocked to see how honest I was with the class when I answered the question about whether I would do anything differently. But as I thought about it, I realized something beautiful and very meaningful to me. I think that I was so open because I was connecting to the students so well, and the reason I was connecting to them was that they had connected to my people. And when I write, I connect to my people so much that I kind of *fuse* with them. So the students connecting with them, connecting with me, made me *fuse* with the students in a profound way. In fact, I remember feeling sad when the video conference was over. I felt there was so much more I wanted to tell them. And have them tell or ask me. Thank you so much for letting me and my people be part of this process.

Reflecting on Your Learning

How might epitextual analysis be used in encouraging students to compare two biographies on the same subject? Is the epitext for nonfiction different in any ways from that for fiction? If so, in what ways? How might epitextual analysis be useful in helping students understand the difference between primary and secondary sources? How might it be useful in helping students understand a nonfiction writer's research process?

References

Alexander, J. (1998). Planning an infinite stay. *New York Times*, Nov. 27. http://movies2.nytimes.com/books/98/09/27/reviews/980927.27alexant.html

Heiligman, D. (2018). YALSA Excellence in Nonfiction awards speech. http://www.ala.org/yalsa/sites/ala.org.yalsa/files/content/booklistsawards/bookawards/margaretaedwards/HEILIGMAN%20YALSA%20EXCELLENCE%20IN%20NONFICTION%20TALK%20FINAL.pdf

Hoffman, P. (1998). *The man who loved only numbers: The story of Paul Erdős and the search for mathematical truth*. New York: Hachette Books.

International Literacy Association. (2015). *Collaborating for success: The vital role of content teachers in developing disciplinary literacy with students in grades 6–12*. [Position statement]. Newark, DE: Author.

Kane, S. (2020). *Integrating literature in the disciplines: Enhancing adolescent learning and literacy, 2d ed.* New York: Routledge.

McLean, D. (1972). "Vincent." United Artists Records, BGO Records.

Rosenblatt, L. (1978). *The reader, the text, the poem: The transactional theory of the literary work*. Carbondale, IL: Southern Illinois University Press.

Sanders, J. S. (2018). *A literature of questions: Nonfiction for the critical child*. Minneapolis: University of Minnesota Press.

Witte, S., Latham, D., & Gross, M. (2019). *Literacy engagement through peritextual analysis*. Chicago: ALA Editions.

Literature Cited

Benjamin, A. (2015). *The thing about jellyfish*. New York: Little, Brown.

Haddon, M. (2003). *The curious incident of the dog in the night-time*. New York: Doubleday.

Heiligman, D. (2009). *Charles and Emma: The Darwins' leap of faith.* New York: Henry Holt.

Heiligman, D. (2013). *The boy who loved math: The improbable life of Paul Erdős.* New York: Roaring Brook Press.

Heiligman, D. (2017). *Vincent and Theo: The Van Gogh brothers.* New York: Henry Holt.

Heiligman, D. (2019). *Torpedoed: The true story of the World War II sinking of "The Children's Ship."* New York: Macmillan.

Heiligman, D. *The girl who loved science: Barbara McClintock.* In preparation.

Montgomery, S. (2015). *The soul of an octopus: A surprising exploration into the wonder of consciousness.* New York: Atria Books.

Montgomery, S., & Green, R. (2018). *How to be a good creature: A memoir in thirteen animals.* Houghton Mifflin Harcourt.

Nelson, M. (2015). *My Seneca Village.* N.p.: Namelos.

Nielsen, S. (2015). *We are all made of molecules.* New York: Wendy Lamb Books.

Polisner, G. (2018). *In sight of stars.* New York: Wednesday Books.

Schwartz, D. M. (1998). *G is for googol: A math alphabet book.* Berkeley, CA: Tricycle Press.

Vanderpool, C. (2013). *Navigating Early.* New York: Delacorte.

Incorporating Epitext Through a Layered-Literacies Approach

Revisiting the Study of *Maus*

Luke Rodesiler and Eric Federspiel

Maus: A Survivor's Tale (1986), a Pulitzer Prize winner in 1992, is the true story of one Holocaust survivor's experience in World War II (WWII) Europe, told via the medium of comics. Writer/artist Art Spiegelman, using hours of interviews with his father as his primary resource, details the horrors and triumphs of his parents' experience in concentration camps and his own challenges in retelling such an important story. The metatextual elements included in *Maus* provide insight into the creative process that students may benefit greatly from—a creative process that is further elucidated via *MetaMaus: A Look Inside a Modern Classic* (Spiegelman, 2011).

In *MetaMaus*, Spiegelman shares with readers never-before-seen photographs, sketches, notes, and scores of other primary documents that give readers of the original work unparalleled access to the process by which Spiegelman crafted his magnum opus. The bonus DVD included with

MetaMaus includes hours of additional source material, including the actual audio recordings from Spiegelman's interviews with his father. With sections devoted to Spiegelman's creative choices, his artistic process, his family history, and the critical reception to the publication of *Maus*, *MetaMaus* fosters a dynamic appreciation of the artistic endeavor. It is therefore easy to see how the use of *MetaMaus* offers educators and librarians an opportunity to take a nuanced approach to the study of *Maus*, which is particularly valuable when it comes to the more challenging aspects of the original work.

Statement of the Problem

Any study of Holocaust literature comes with its own unique set of challenges. Unlike studying many other texts in the traditional literary canon, reading Holocaust literature requires a fairly thorough understanding of world events up to and including WWII in order to fully comprehend the magnitude of the Holocaust. In some circumstances, educators and librarians may find themselves responsible for providing this historical context, which requires a significant amount of preparation. Students with little exposure to anti-Semitism might also find the events in Holocaust literature difficult to grasp, especially in terms of the scale and sheer brutality inflicted upon European Jews. Without the capacity to empathize with the plight of Spiegelman's father and all Holocaust victims and survivors, readers risk missing much of the emotional resonance of *Maus*.

> Young people can grapple with difficult topics when given the right care and scaffolding. Texts such as *Maus* can teach all of us about resilience in spite of difficult situations.

Additionally, the topic of the Holocaust is one that students, educators, and librarians may find disturbing. By its very nature, Holocaust literature describes events and ideas often considered taboo in secondary schools, such as religion, nudity, violence, and death. It is easy to see how students, educators, and librarians may find *Maus*, which contains *visual* representations of these taboo events and ideas, too disturbing for use in the classroom. But however tempting it might be to protect students from potentially troubling topics—such as the events of the Holocaust—denying them access to such topics also shields them from history. Engaging with such topics in the safety of the classroom can help to establish schools as "places where young people can face troubling content with caring teachers" (Chisholm & Whitmore, 2018, p. 10).

The medium in which Spiegelman's father's story is told—comics—may be unfamiliar to many high school students, making it another aspect of *Maus* that may pose challenges. Though the popularity of graphic novels in school libraries and superhero adventures on the silver screen might suggest otherwise, comics remain a fairly niche medium, particularly in terms of use in English language arts classrooms. As a result, many students simply lack exposure to the mechanics of graphic storytelling. Obviously, reading traditional prose can be challenging in and of itself. But without prior experience with comics, readers of *Maus* may find themselves lost on the page, unable to identify which panel comes after which, or which character is speaking. Additionally, many educators lack experience using comics to support teaching and learning, requiring additional instructional preparation that the study of traditional prose does not.

When used as a supplement to the original work, *MetaMaus* can help to address these challenges. Photographs that capture the horrors faced by concentration camp prisoners help students to connect historical events with the experiences of real people. Audio recordings of Spiegelman's father illustrate the difficulty of living with painful memories. Interviews with Spiegelman's wife and children help students comprehend the legacy of anti-Semitism. Finally, description of Spiegelman's creative choices when designing page layouts helps students understand the visual language of comics while fostering an appreciation for the unique benefits of the medium. For these reasons (among others), *MetaMaus* is an extremely valuable resource that can help students to gain a more intimate, personal view of both the creation of *Maus* and the Holocaust in general.

The use of *Maus* and *MetaMaus* also allows educators and librarians to address challenges with Holocaust literature typically taught in secondary classrooms, which can be either too narrowly focused (e.g., *Anne Frank: The Diary of a Young Girl* [1952/1993]) or too challenging for developing readers and writers (e.g., *Night* [Wiesel, 1960/1986]). *Maus* and *MetaMaus* are unique in that they, by nature of their formats, provide visual and auditory support that can benefit all students and especially those who may struggle with reading comprehension. There is evidence that the visuals themselves "can serve as indicators of what is important in the written text, and can assist readers by focusing attention on specific ideas" (Cook, 2017, p. 27). Even if some students may struggle with the broken English used by Spiegelman's father Vladek, the artwork is always there as a safety net, making the text that

> Multimodal epitexts such as MetaMaus bring dimension and perspective to comprehension and critical thinking.

much more accessible. The audio recordings of interviews conducted with Spiegelman's father in *MetaMaus* are also accessible to students regardless of their reading proficiency, providing another entry point to the study of *Maus* itself.

Theoretical Framework

Gérard Genette's (1991) definition of paratext accounts for two components, each of which informs how readers make sense of a given text: *peritext* and *epitext*. According to Genette, peritext includes the elements "around the text, in the space of the same volume" (p. 263). A text's title, table of contents, preface, dust jacket, and the like fall into this category. Distinguished from peritext by proximity to the text, epitext, as Genette explained, includes elements that "are situated, at least originally, outside the book" (p. 264). For example, interviews or other correspondence with the author and author diaries or journal entries would be categorized as epitext. Taken together, peritext and epitext constitute paratext.

See the introduction to this book for a full explanation of the functions of epitext and Chapter 1 for an overview of epitextual analysis.

Building from Genette's (1991) concept of paratext, Gross and Latham (2017) advanced the peritextual literacy framework (PLF) as "a tool for accessing, evaluating, and comprehending the content of media using elements that frame the body of a work and mediate its content for the user" (p. 116). Building on the PLF, epitextual analysis can assist readers in utilizing epitextual elements to support meaning making. Epitextual analysis accounts for up to six functional types of epitext: production, promotion, dissemination, reception, extension, and referential. This chapter focuses on using production-based epitext, which includes texts spatially removed from a given work yet still pertinent to the various stages of that work's production (i.e., pre-, during, and post-production), to support literacy teaching and learning.

Specifically, this chapter envisions how the study of production-based epitext can enhance an approach to literature study that involves "layering literacies" (Chisholm & Whitmore, 2018, p. 5). Rather than conceptualizing literacy narrowly, the approach embraces multimodal social semiotic theories (see, for example, Kress & van Leeuwen, 2001) and the range of modes people use daily to make meaning. Recognizing a multitude of literacies, Chisholm and Whitmore (2018) advocated for helping students *see* the text, *be* the text, and *feel* the text over the course of a unit. Each layer is valuable in its own right, and collectively a layered-literacies approach stands to offer students a rich learning experience.

When helping students *see* the text, educators and librarians support them in developing visual literacies (Chisholm & Whitmore, 2018). Such work involves fostering students' capacities to read the grammar of visual design, including structures outlined by Serafini (2011):

1. composition, or how objects are arranged in a visual image;

2. perspective, including how close or distant subjects in an image appear and how they are positioned in relation to one another (and to the reader); and

3. visual symbols, which artists use to depict ideas "conventionalized through their use in sociocultural contexts" (p. 346).

Accounting for students' visual literacies is especially necessary when inviting them to read texts featured in the unit described here: comics.

Teaching that involves helping students *be* the text fosters embodied literacies (Chisholm & Whitmore, 2018). When educators and librarians use enactment strategies such as those Wilhelm (2008) described, students use their bodies to make meaning of written texts while also becoming texts to be read by others. For instance, when creating tableaux, frozen physical depictions of story scenes, students are challenged to consider and convey through body positioning and facial expressions their interpretations of a text. Likewise, analogy dramas, in which students create and perform original vignettes mirroring story situations, and dramatic play, in which students take on roles of story characters and imagine and enact how they would respond to story events, are examples of enactment strategies that can support the development of embodied literacies.

When educators and librarians help students *feel* the text, they are nurturing emotional literacies (Chisholm & Whitmore, 2018). Accounting for students' emotional literacies has multiple benefits, as Chisholm and Whitmore (2018) explained: "Emotionally mediated literacy experiences allow one to imagine the context of another, thereby providing multiple perspectives on texts and the capacity to draw on those perspectives to act in the world" (p. 60). Emotional literacies are particularly valuable when reading a challenging text featuring content that, given its incredible gravity, begs to be acted upon in the present day. Spiegelman's *Maus* is one such text.

Relevant Literature

Research suggests that successfully reading comics such as *Maus* requires significant work on the part of the reader. In a study investigating how the features of a graphic novel work together to tell a story and what readers must notice to understand them, Smith and Pole (2018) emphasized the complexity of sequential art. Focusing on the award-winning graphic novel *El Deafo* (Bell, 2014), the researchers described complexity in the interrelation between words and illustrations, in the text within speech balloons, and in the use of color and line. Subsequently, they advised educators to be intentional about teaching students to read visuals; this includes using instructional methods such as creating anchor charts to document visual features and the purposes they serve in graphic novels, as well as facilitating mini-lessons about reading specific visuals. Smith and Pole also argued that, despite graphic novels having a reputation as quick reads, the multimodal components of graphic novels necessitate slow reading that allows for peering across and within frames, studying color and line, inferring meaning, and making other moves to support comprehension. Further, the researchers stressed the value of readers talking with others about graphic novels to support meaning-making. These findings are in line with those of researchers who contend that reading graphic novels requires specialized knowledge (e.g., Jiménez & Meyer, 2016), and they inform the layered-literacies instructional approach described later in this chapter, which incorporates epitext to support the study of *Maus* in the secondary English language arts classroom.

Context

Sadly, the recent rise of hate crimes (Faupel, Scheuerman, Parris, & Werum, 2019), mass shootings, and anti-Semitism in the United States may provide students with a context for the tragic events of the Holocaust that they might otherwise be missing. Students will more than likely be familiar with events such as the 2018 shooting at Marjory Stoneman Douglas High School in Parkland, Florida, particularly because 14 of the victims were high school students themselves. The activism of student survivors in the wake of the shooting may provide a touchstone for classroom conversations about the power that young people have to respond to tragedy.

The deadly attack at the Tree of Life Synagogue in Pittsburgh on October 27, 2018, is clear evidence that though the events of *Maus* occurred more than 70 years ago, religious discrimination is still a very real and dangerous problem today. In fact, according to the Anti-Defamation

League (2019), Jews and Jewish institutions across the United States faced 1,879 attacks in 2018, with instances of assault up dramatically from the previous year. For this reason, there is perhaps no better time for students to engage with texts like *Maus* and *MetaMaus*, which provide historical and personal evidence of the danger of hate unchecked on a global scale.

In light of recent hateful attacks in the United States, the authors of this chapter—an English teacher educator (Rodesiler) and an instructional designer (Federspiel)—

> Though some critics suggest that Holocaust literature is irrelevant to today's adolescents, we are steadfast in providing opportunities for all to learn from the mistakes of the past. Deep readings of texts and epitexts help bring perspective to our current world climate.

were moved to reflect upon their respective experiences teaching Holocaust literature as high school English teachers. Specifically, the authors set out to draw upon recent scholarship promoting the role epitext can play in advancing literature study and the potential of a layered-literacies approach as they re-envisioned instructional methods for engaging students with such challenging texts and tough topics.

Practical Methods

Rich with insights about the production of Spiegelman's award-winning comic, *MetaMaus* offers epitext that educators and librarians can use to help students *see* the text, *be* the text, and *feel* the text that is *Maus*. The practical methods described

> We love the idea that epitext can help students *see* the text, *be* the text, and *feel* the text.

here illustrate ways that purposefully drawing from *MetaMaus* can support a layered-literacies approach to the study of Spiegelman's award-winning comic.

Seeing the Text

Rather than thrust comics upon students without attending to their needs related to reading the grammar of visual design, educators and librarians can use excerpts from *MetaMaus* to support them. For example, a chapter titled "Why Mice?" gives students a chance to learn about prominent symbols in *Maus*, including the cat-mouse metaphor of oppression in which mice represent Jews and cats represent Nazis. In that chapter, Spiegelman (2011) points to the role that dehumanization efforts—including the production and distribution of propaganda that portrayed Jews as rats swarming in a sewer—played in the Holocaust: "Dehumanization is just basic to the whole killing project . . . The idea of Jews as toxic, as disease carriers, as dangerous subhuman creatures, was a necessary prerequisite for killing my family" (p. 115). With such passages, "Why Mice?" can help students learn not only about visual symbols but also about anti-Semitism and the role of dehumanization in attacks made against entire ethnic groups.

For students who are inexperienced in reading comics, *MetaMaus* offers opportunities to learn straight from the author/illustrator about the purposeful use of panels. Spiegelman (2011) clarifies his intentional choices, explaining, "And the size of a panel was of utmost importance, whether a picture takes up a half a page, a third of a page, or is part of a row of narrow boxes has meaning" (p. 175). Such passages invite students to consider why Spiegelman framed particular scenes in the narrative as he did. For instance, students can discuss the significance of using a half-page image on page 34 to show young Vladek and Anja first seeing a swastika and weigh the gravity conveyed by making the image of their arrival at the gates of Auschwitz bleed off the page at the end of the volume. Further, when attending to framing, students can also explore the use of overtly symbolic panels, such as on page 82, where the star of David frames young Vladek as he contemplates whether to walk or run from a scene where Jews are under attack.

Excerpts from *MetaMaus* can also help students build visual literacy as it pertains to reading other compositional elements of *Maus*, such as the use of circular motifs. As Spiegelman (2011) explains, "Circular motifs do have a privileged role in the book, if nothing else, because it's integral to the swastika logo-design. . . . And, of course, circles are always useful for focusing meaning" (pp. 182–183). Knowing that the author/illustrator was intentional in his use of circles, students can spend more time reading panels in which circles appear and consider how they contribute to the meaning readers make, whether considering how they frame the swastika "as a kind of a moon" (Spiegelman, 2011, p. 183) hanging over the proceedings on page 35 of *Maus*, weighing how they give emphasis to threats made against young Vladek and others upon arriving at a prisoner-of-war camp on page 53, or thinking through other instances in which the circular motif appears in the comic.

Being the Text

Part of the power of the visuals in *Maus* is that they help students visualize life (and death) in the concentration camps without subjecting them to graphic photographs that could "result in students quickly distancing themselves from those who perpetrated, assisted, and stood by while others succumbed to, suffered through, and actively fought against genocide" (Chisholm & Whitmore, 2018, p. 21). At the same time, the anthropomorphizing of the camp prisoners may inhibit students' ability to understand the physical and emotional scale of human suffering that took place during and as a result of the Holocaust. By engaging in classroom activities that encourage students to *be* the text, students can use their own physical bodies to address that challenge.

Through the embodied strategy of "Tableau," which encourages dramatic physical enactment to retell scenes from the text, students place themselves in the shoes of Spiegelman's father, echoing "our collective pedagogical call to enter into the study of the Holocaust one person, one emotion, at a time" (Chisholm & Whitmore, 2018, p. 39). Like Spiegelman's mouse mask, this activity allows students to engage with the plight of the characters of *Maus* while avoiding the suggestion that there is any way to truly comprehend what it must have been like to live through the Holocaust. In the words of Spiegelman's father, "About Auschwitz, nobody can understand" (Spiegelman, 1986, p. 224).

In Tableau, a small group of two or three students creates a silent "frozen picture" using only their bodies for props. Using the reference photo for the cover of *Maus* as featured in *MetaMaus* (p. 78) as a starting point, educators and librarians can invite students to physically create alternative book jacket covers for *Maus*. By quickly planning out their performance beforehand and embodying an important scene or thematic connection to the text, students become the text, sharing their interpretations with the "audience" of their classmates. After their performances, students can explain the scenes they chose to reenact, providing reasoning for why their chosen scenes might serve as appropriate representations of *Maus* as a whole.

Spiegelman's (2011) explanation of his choice to use very few photographs in *Maus* (pp. 218–224, 232) can serve as inspiration for another tableau, in which students illustrate other important—if not book jacket cover-worthy—scenes from *Maus*. Educators and librarians could capture photographs of the students' tableaux for closer post-performance inspection or even display the photographs for others to see, which would extend the embodied approach to include *seeing* the text (Chisholm & Whitmore, 2018).

Feeling the Text

When facilitating the study of *Maus*, educators and librarians can further layer literacies by incorporating epitext and facilitating activities aimed at eliciting emotional responses, helping students view through an affective lens the Holocaust and its devastating effects on Spiegelman's family and countless others. Educators and librarians can use multiple methods to tap students' emotions in ways that help them contextualize the Holocaust and connect with their local community in remembrance and in hope for a brighter future. When incorporating excerpts from *MetaMaus* as epitext, such methods can include students examining Vladek's eyewitness accounts via audio-recorded interviews and corresponding transcripts before reproducing passages of those interviews for public reflection.

Inviting living Holocaust survivors into the school to share their stories can make for an emotional experience; however, doing so is not always feasible. Alternatively, educators and librarians can help students contextualize the Holocaust and the events depicted in *Maus* specifically by pulling from *MetaMaus* and its supplementary files audio recordings and corresponding transcripts documenting Spiegelman's foundational interviews with his father. The interviews are wide-ranging, including Vladek's recollection of meeting and marrying Anja, reporting for duty at the war's onset, being forced into labor as a prisoner of war, witnessing unspeakable cruelty and anticipating his own demise in Auschwitz, and much more. The audio recordings of Vladek's voice, pained by the traumas he experienced, appropriately contextualize the events described, helping students to feel the gravity of the circumstances and the weight of his suffering.

After listening to the interviews, students may be eager to help others connect with the experiences Vladek shared. Chisholm and Whitmore (2018) described teachers and students reproducing on the marquee in front of their school meaningful passages from *Anne Frank: The Diary of a Young Girl*. It was an intentional effort to go public with Frank's words and encourage the community's collective reflection upon her message. Likewise, educators and librarians can invite students to reproduce Vladek's evocative words and take his message to the local community. Students can select short passages that moved them and, in turn, may prompt passers-by to remember and reflect. For example, students might identify short yet stirring excerpts from the interviews published in *MetaMaus* (Spiegelman, 2011), including ". . . and every day was for us a year" (p. 241); "We were together and we survived" (p. 241); "It was forty thousand Jews in Sosnowiec, maybe we had only five thousand left" (p. 246); and "Let's hope this will not repeat" (p. 277). Publicly displaying words that evoke feelings among students has the potential to nudge the entire community into reflecting upon the tremendous hardships Vladek and millions more experienced, while helping to protect against a dark chapter of history being forgotten or repeated.

Conclusion

The challenges of engaging students in the study of *Maus,* described at the beginning of this chapter, were easily identified because they were difficulties that one co-author experienced personally when first incorporating excerpts of the popular comic in an English language arts course for high school freshmen deemed "at risk." This chapter provided a space for sharing a reconceptualization of his instructional methods, a revision shaped by epitextual analysis and a layered-literacies approach to facilitating literature study.

Applied in tandem, epitextual analysis and a layered-literacies approach offer a way to extend students' comprehension and to support the development of multiple literacies, including the visual, the embodied, and the emotional. In the face of unique difficulties that arise with the study of challenging texts and the tough topics they address, such as death, religion, and genocide, educators and librarians can draw upon epitext to deepen their own understandings and to supplement student learning. Considering *MetaMaus* in relation to *Maus: A Survivor's Tale* offers a prime example of rich production-based epitext that, when used purposefully, can help educators, librarians, and students build knowledge about everything from the corresponding text's compositional elements and visual symbols to its historical context and the sociocultural circumstances in which the events therein unfolded.

Reflecting on Your Learning

In what ways does epitext help students *see* the text, *be* the text, and *feel* the text? How can you use epitext to build dimensional and critical-thinking scaffolds to a core text?

References

Anti-Defamation League. (2019). *Audit of anti-Semitic incidents: Year in review 2018*. https://www.adl.org/media/12857/download

Bell, C. (2014). *El deafo*. New York: Amulet.

Chisholm, J. S., & Whitmore, K. F. (2018). *Reading challenging texts: Layering literacies through the arts*. New York: Routledge.

Cook, M. P. (2017). Now I "see": The impact of graphic novels on reading comprehension in high school English classrooms. *Literacy Research and Instruction, 56*(1): 21–53.

Faupel, A., Scheuerman, H. L., Parris, C. L., & Werum, R. (2019, August 13). Hate crimes are on the rise. What does it take to get state governments to respond? *The Washington Post.* https://www.washingtonpost.com/politics/2019/08/13/hate-crimes-are-rise-what-does-it-take-get-state-governments-respond

Frank, A. (1952/1993). *Anne Frank: The diary of a young girl.* New York: Bantam Books.

Genette, G. (1991). Introduction to the paratext. *New Literary History, 22*(2): 261–272.

Gross, M., & Latham, D. (2017). The peritextual literacy framework: Using the functions of peritext to support critical thinking. *Library and Information Science Research, 39*: 116–123.

Jiménez, L. M., & Meyer, C. K. (2016). First impressions matter: Navigating graphic novels utilizing linguistic, visual, and spatial resources. *Journal of Literacy Research, 48*(4): 423–447.

Kress, G., & van Leeuwen, T. (2001). *Multimodal discourse.* London, UK: Arnold.

Serafini, F. (2011). Expanding perspectives for comprehending visual images in multimodal texts. *Journal of Adolescent & Adult Literacy, 54*(5): 342–350.

Smith, J. M., & Pole, K. (2018). What's going on in a graphic novel? *The Reading Teacher, 72*(2): 169–177.

Spiegelman, A. (1986). *Maus: A survivor's tale.* New York: Pantheon Books.

Spiegelman, A. (2011). *MetaMaus: A look inside a modern classic.* New York: Pantheon Books.

Wiesel, E. (1960/1986). *Night.* New York: Bantam Books.

Wilhelm, J. D. (2008). *"You gotta be the book": Teaching engaged and reflective reading with adolescents* (2d ed.). New York: Teachers College Press.

CHAPTER 4

Learning Through Fan Fiction

Remix and Extension with Narrative Writing

Tyler C. Sisco

Fan fiction. People who know what it is probably have strong feelings about it. Writing purists may scoff at these fan-made works. Concerned parents may worry about what their children are reading online, as these pieces sometimes include adult content or remix characters from texts of varying age appropriateness. People who love to read or write fan fiction know that it can be a cognitively complex task to write stories using someone else's work as a basis. Other fans are happy to point out perceived mistakes in interpretation. Arguments over whether or not a certain character would make a certain decision in this fan-made scenario often ensue, and the participants may not be aware of how deeply they are analyzing the works they have read—all in the name of

> Passionate arguments among fan-fiction writers can be seen as examples of reception epitext— reception of both the original text and the fan fiction inspired by that text.

fandom and fun. What would happen, then, if one could apply aspects of fandom culture to a secondary English classroom?

Statement of Issue to Be Considered

Most English Language Arts (ELA) standards, at all grade levels, including the Common Core, can be grouped into three categories: Reading, Writing, and, to a lesser extent, Speaking and Listening. All skills that ELA teachers teach come from one of those categories.

When planning units that involve reading lengthy texts, such as novels, it can be difficult to incorporate an adequate amount of writing that is relevant to the text. Too often, teachers fall back on argumentative response essays as a way to ask students to write about what they have read, but that type of work fails to engage the creative aspects of the minds of students. Asking students to write an essay analyzing whether or not George did the right thing by killing Lennie in *Of Mice and Men* (Steinbeck, 1937) is a good exercise in essay writing, morality, and argument, but does not directly ask students to delve into the themes of the novel, explore the impact of side characters, or analyze the structure of the novel.

The use of epitext, which consists of elements that are developed outside of a text but are related to and supportive of the central text, can provide additional methods for unifying the teaching of reading and writing. Specifically, this chapter discusses the use of extension texts to increase engagement and allow for greater creativity and flexibility when planning units that involve reading and writing. Extension texts come in a variety of formats, including fan fiction, prequels and sequels, and remixes.

How the Work Is Situated in Epitext

There are three important questions to consider when examining extension texts:

These questions are also presented in the introduction to this book.

- How do these texts help you understand the work better?

- How do readers of a work interact with the work?

- How does the creation of extension texts honor or critique the work?

Understanding a work is a core goal of reading instruction. Extension epitext can help students understand the characters of the main text by asking them to accurately portray those characters in a new scenario. Students must adequately understand characters to be able to judge how they would react under new circumstances. Extension asks students to recreate aspects of a text, such as detailed descriptions of settings or the style of the author's language. This mimicry requires students to dissect and interact closely with the text, leading to deeper understanding.

These extensions can honor or critique the main text through the creative choices of the student author. Students who choose to write an extension that is entirely true to the main text, almost like a deleted scene from a film, may feel like the main text is great as it already is. They are honoring the text. Students who feel like the main text has major flaws could choose to make changes to aspects of the text, such as adding a more diverse character. This could be applied to many commonly taught, but often debated, texts in American classrooms. For example, the novel

> Rosenblatt (1978) identified two kinds of reading—efferent and aesthetic. (For more information, see Kane & Heiligman's chapter in this book.) How might students' extensions of a text reflect these two kinds of reading of the text?

To Kill a Mockingbird by Harper Lee (1960) is considered by many to be an essential classic, taught typically around the eighth or ninth grade. A student writing an extension could honor the text by rewriting a scene from the text through the point of view of Boo Radley instead of Scout. This fits with the novel's theme of seeing multiple perspectives. A student critiquing the text could write a scene where Scout sneaks into a side room while at church with Calpurnia (something that fits with Scout's character), and then overhears African American characters expressing frustration that they need to rely on a White man to save a member of their community from injustice. This would be an example of the "White Savior" critique that the novel commonly receives.

Review of the Relevant Literature

Fan fiction is sometimes misunderstood and underestimated by people who are unfamiliar with it, but creating it is a challenging and creative task. McWilliams, Hickey, Hines, Conner, and Bishop (2011) note, "Fan fiction communities are known for their deep engagement with and close reading of source material;—practices that align closely with the goals of many Language Arts teachers" (p. 241). In fan fiction, the writer must understand the characters and settings of the story well enough to make a believable addition to the original story. For example, a study by Jen Curwood (2013) noted that a young fan-fiction writer "had to build on textual evidence and consider how her assigned character . . . might change when he was put in life threatening circumstances" (p. 86).

A great deal of fan fiction commonly found on the Internet is based on popular young adult literature. However, any text can be the source for extension using fan fiction or a similar technique. Even texts considered part of the literary canon can be extended by student writers using fan fiction. Secondary students often feel disconnected from the literary canon typically taught in high school classrooms, and it is no mystery why. The works of Shakespeare are one example of this. England in the fifteenth century was a vastly different place, with very different people, from a modern American city. ELA teachers can help students make connections with texts in the literary canon, but a true test of students' understanding of the themes, characters, and settings of a text can be accomplished through extension. In 2018, a group of ninth-grade students in a Midwestern city did just that, with John Steinbeck's *Of Mice and Men* (1937).

Context

This project was completed by ninth-grade students in a public school located in a large metropolitan area of a Midwestern city in the United States. According to the State Department of Education 2017–2018 Report Card, the district has more than 22,000 students enrolled. The high school these students attended had just over 1,000 students in grades 9–12. In that school year, 49.95% of the students at this high school were African American, 19.58% were Hispanic, and 16.07% were White. Eighty percent were economically disadvantaged. Eighteen percent were English Language Learners (ELL), and 17.27% were students with disabilities. The graduation rate was 76.7%. Their attendance rates and ACT scores were lower than the state average (Anonymous State Department of Education, 2019).

I (the author of this chapter) am also a second-year teacher who created this project and implemented it. Although I collaborate in a professional learning community with two other grade-level English teachers, I was the primary creator of the project highlighted in this chapter. The school did not have advanced placement or honors courses, so almost all ninth-grade students were in mixed-ability classes. Two of the class periods had a Special Education (SPED) co-teacher. Classes met for 90 minutes twice a week, and 45 minutes one day per week. Most students were provided laptops through the school for a small fee. Many strategies and technologies were used throughout the semester in the classroom, including exit tickets; a vocabulary Word of the Week; and notes delivered through Google Slides, Google Classroom, Kahoot!, and Flipgrid. No smartboard was available, but there was a projector. *Of Mice and Men* (Steinbeck, 1937) was the first novel they read as a class that semester. They read it during the month of October, at the beginning of Quarter Two. In the previous quarter, students had received instruction focused on persuasion and argument writing.

Application of Approach

The project was called the "Unseen Scene Project." This chapter includes actual documents that were used in this project, to help guide anyone who wishes to use extension or remix in their own classroom. Figure 4-1 is part of the assignment introduction that was used with the project. It defines the requirements and goal of the assignment. Students were supposed to create an alternate scene, a scene that occurred "off-screen," or a flashback.

NARRATIVE WRITING: AN UNSEEN SCENE

You have finished reading John Steinbeck's *Of Mice and Men*. We have learned about text structure, author's choices, and figurative language. Now, you will add your own story to this great work of literature. You will produce an "unseen scene" from OM&M. This could be:

- **an alternate scene**
  - ○ Like the alternate ending we watched from SNL, write a scene from the novel, but with a twist. Something changed. Something is different, and it changes everything else.
- **OR a scene that happens "off-screen"**
  - ○ Where the author focused on one thing happening to just some characters, but other characters were off doing something else. You tell us what happened to the characters we didn't get to read about.
- **OR a flashback**
  - ○ Something talked about during the novel, but it happened before the beginning.

Figure 4-1: Unseen Scene Assignment Introduction.

Popular alternate scenes included ones where Curley's wife did not die or Lennie escaped in the end. The most common off-screen scenes were ones addressing the death of Candy's dog or what the other characters were doing when Lennie killed Curley's wife. Several students created a flashback scene to a past incident that George mentions where Lennie inappropriately touched a woman and it caused them to be chased out of town. In each of these cases, the students had to deeply analyze the plot structure, character motivations, and language to realistically recreate or alter the story. (All names used in this chapter are pseudonyms to protect the privacy of the students.)

In this example, an ELL and SPED student named Shen wrote an alternate ending to *Of Mice and Men* where Lennie escapes death:

> "I will run away," Lennie said.
>
> He was planning to go to the city and try to survive and not to be killed by George. While he was running away he heard a creepy sound coming from the forest which made him a little scared because he might be eaten up when he was running he was thinking about the bad decision that he kill Curley wife. [*sic*]

This example shows that Shen understands the important characteristics of Lennie: he does not seek out violence, but instead runs away. He did not want to kill anyone, and feels guilty for his actions. He is childlike and afraid of the noises in the dark. Some of Shen's classmates thought that Lennie was evil after finishing the book, and they did not understand that he was trying to avoid violence. Shen struggled to understand Lennie at first, too. However, through the writing process, he was able to explore Lennie's character to produce a better extension scene.

Students interact with the text in a variety of ways when engaging in extension. Another student, Casey, wrote the scene where Candy shoots his old dog. In the novel, we only hear the gunshot, but Casey felt that the scene would have been more powerful if we had been able to see it. One class, including a student named Amelia, felt it was strange that none of the men playing horseshoes came to help or heard Curley's wife screaming. She wrote a scene explaining how this could have happened. One of Amelia's classmates, Maria, wrote an alternate ending where Curley's wife kills Lennie instead:

> She tries to run back but as soon as she gets to the door Lennie pulls on her hair and tries to grab her arms. Curley's wife terrifyingly looks around and sees a gun hanging from the barn door, she rapidly yanks her hair out of Lennie's hands and shoves him away.

"If you take a step any closer I will shoot you! I ain't gonna have no mercy for you boy!"

Lennie lowers his head and whispers "George can't know . . . Nobody can know." He suddenly raises his head and shouts "I can't be lettin' you tell him!"

Curley's wife panics and pulls the trigger.

Maria's example, as well as Casey's and Amelia's, shows that extension can also help students critique or honor the literary work. Steinbeck's novel has often received criticism for its portrayal of women. Maria's scene ends with Curley's wife running away to pursue her own dreams. She wrote, "All that is on her mind is . . . what will her new beginning look like?" If the novel had actually ended that way, its central themes would have been significantly different.

One example of a flashback comes from Bella. At the end of her scene, she uses repetition to really connect her versions of Lennie and George to the characters in the original text:

"Oh Lennie I know you didn't mean any harm, but you really have to be careful and think about what you're doing."

"I know George, it's just the dress looked really soft. I'm not gonna get to tend no rabbits now."

"That's not true Lennie, it was an accident. You're still gonna get to tend the rabbits."

"Really George? Oh thank you, I won't do anything like that again George."

"Good Lennie, I hope you don't."

Throughout the novel, Lennie repeatedly is motivated by his desire to care for small furry creatures. Using that detail in her scene helped Bella accurately portray this dialogue between Lennie and George. She also uses foreshadowing with the line "I won't do anything like that again George." This shows that Bella has an even deeper understanding of the text than what was required for this project.

The students were able to choose how to demonstrate their knowledge during the project. They could write the story in a traditional format, typed in a document (WRITE IT);

> If time permits, students could produce more than one format of their story, and thus explore the opportunities offered and issues raised in trying to produce transmedia.

OPTION 1: WRITE IT Rubric
- **Final Draft Due November 23, 11:59 pm (50 performance points)**
  - ○ Grammar/Spelling/Mechanics (10 points)
  - ○ Based in the novel (10 points)
  - ○ Appropriate mix of dialogue and description (5 points)
  - ○ Is an unseen scene, flashback, or alternate ending (10 points)
  - ○ Appropriate length of at least 500 words (5 points)
  - ○ Follows a narrative story arc (10 points)

OPTION 2: DRAW IT Rubric
- **Final Draft Due November 20, 3 pm (50 performance points)**
  - ○ Grammar/Spelling/Mechanics (5 points)
  - ○ Use of images to convey meaning (5 points)
  - ○ Use of dialogue to convey meaning (5 points)
  - ○ Based in the novel (10 points)
  - ○ Is an unseen scene, flashback, or alternate ending (10 points)
  - ○ Follows a narrative story arc (10 points)
  - ○ Appropriate length of at least 15 panels (5 points)

Figure 4-2: Option 1: WRITE IT Rubric.

create a comic or graphic story format that incorporated words and images (DRAW IT); create a script for their scene and perform it for the class (ACT IT); or film their scene, edit it in iMovie, and play it for the class on the date it was due (FILM IT). The rubrics for all of these options can be seen in Figures 4-2 and 4-3.

The requirements in the rubrics were based on lessons that were taught leading up to the project. Students completed activities related to narrative structure, descriptive and figurative language, and dialogue. Therefore, those were included in the requirements for the project. Students could work alone or in a small group. Once they decided who they would work with and how they would complete the project, the students filled out a half-page project contract. They had three ninety-minute class periods to complete the project, and were encouraged to work at home if they needed more time. Throughout the process, their teacher supported them

OPTION 3: ACT IT Rubric
- **Final Draft Due November 19/20 during class (50 performance points)**
  - ○ Script (35 points)
    - ■ Spelling/Grammar/Mechanics (5 points)
    - ■ Based in the novel (10 points)
    - ■ Is an unseen scene, flashback, or alternate ending (10 points)
    - ■ Follows a narrative story arc (10 points)
  - ○ Performance (15 points)
    - ■ Speech clear and loud, lines read with dramatic effect (5 points)
    - ■ Props used (5 points)
    - ■ Appropriate length of at least 3 minutes (5 points)

OPTION 4: FILM IT Rubric
- **Final Draft Due November 19/20, end of class (50 performance points)**
  - ○ Grammar/Spelling/Mechanics (5 points)
  - ○ Based in the novel (10 points)
  - ○ Use of dialogue (5 points)
  - ○ Is an unseen scene, flashback, or alternate ending (10 points)
  - ○ Appropriate length of at least 3 minutes (5 points)
  - ○ Follows a narrative story arc (10 points)
  - ○ Film editing is clean and cohesive (5 minutes)

Figure 4-3: Option 3: ACT IT Rubric.

with progress checks, exemplified by Figures 4-4 and 4-5, and step-by-step guides (Figure 4-6).

These progress checks and guides were specific to each project option. Progress checks for FILM IT included a checkpoint date for the script and a checkpoint date for the filming, whereas progress checks for WRITE IT encouraged students to begin by writing dialogue and then adding description later.

The DRAW IT and FILM IT options also had graphic organizers to assist students as they worked. The DRAW IT template shown in Figure 4-7 was

Rough Draft Progress Checks
- ○ November 15/16 start of class (20 practice points)
  - ■ Dialogue should be complete
- ○ November 19/20 start of class (20 practice points)
  - ■ Description and dialogue should be complete

Figure 4-4: An example of the progress checks the teacher implemented for the WRITE IT option.

Rough Draft Progress Checks
- ○ November 15/16 start of class (20 practice points)
  - ■ Script complete
- ○ November 19/20 start of class (20 practice points)
  - ■ Filming complete, ready to edit

Figure 4-5: Rough Draft Progress Checks.

DRAW IT: Steps for Success
1. Complete and turn in Project Contract
2. Complete a panel summary outline
   a. A Panel Summary Outline is just a list of what will be on each panel. Example:
      1. Lennie sits and stares at the dead puppy
      2. Lennie touches the puppy's fur and says "Why do you got to get killed?"
      3...
         (and so on until all your panels/drawings have been planned out)
   b. You will write dialogue in dramatic format as you do this.
   c. Here is a Template for you to copy and use.
3. Ask someone to read your outline (a teacher, friend, and/or other adult)
4. Revise and edit
5. Begin drawing your panels in pencil
6. Check the Rubric to make sure it meets the requirements
7. Go back over your panels and add colors
8. Submit assignment by the deadline

Figure 4-6: DRAW IT: "Steps for Success." This document is an example of the step-by-step guides the teacher created to assist students throughout the process.

To use this template, click "File" ➡ "Make a Copy". Rename the copy with the title of your scene and your name(s). Share it with any other group members. Attach it to the "Narrative Writing Assignment" post on Google Classroom so I can monitor your progress. Delete all the text in red [italic] before final submission.

Panel Summary Outline   Name:

#	Summary	Caption/Dialogue
1	*What will you draw on this panel?*	*What captions or dialogue will be associated with this panel?*
2		
3		
4		
5		
6		
7		
8		
9		
10		
11		
12		
13		
14		
15		

Figure 4-7: This document helped students completing the DRAW IT option to plan their work before they began.

meant to help students separate the dialogue and visual elements of their graphic story. The FILM IT graphic organizer looked similar, but the columns read "Duration: Estimate how long this will take," "Dialogue: What will be said?", and "Scene Description: What will we see on screen?"

One good example of the DRAW IT option came from Jayden and Eric. These students kept their actual graphic story, but the panel summary outline from their planning process can provide enough details about their scene (Figure 4-8). They did an alternate scene where Curley murders his wife and blames it on Lennie.

Panel Summary Outline   Name: Jayden and Eric

#	Summary	Caption/Dialogue
1	Curley's Wife and curly are arguing	
2	She keeps going back and forth with him	
3	He pushes her really hard and she gets knocked out	
4	Curley rushes to see if she is ok	shoot!!!
5	She looks at him confused when she wakes up	What happend i blacked out
6	He tries to comfort her	
7	She feels assaulted	
8	She pushes him off her	
9	He grabes a crowbar and beats her with it	
10	She is not moving, she dies	
11	Curley is worried	
12	He things of a way to get out of it	He knows she is dead
13	He stands there and say's to himself	"Lennie"
14	He could blame the whole thing on Lennie	
15	He stands there for a second	He thinks of a story to tell
16	We see an alternate reality where Lennie kills Curley's Wife	So he could say he heard her sceaming for help and that he saw her laying on the ground next to lennie dead
17	He stands there and smile	He had it all planned out
18	So he left to find Lennie	
19	He told him to go in and get a ranch out of the barn	
20	Lennie did as told and lenni went in there and he saw her and try to wake her up then Curly came in and said you Monster	Curleys plan was all set

Figure 4-8: A completed DRAW IT outline from Jayden and Eric. After they made this outline, they drew the final product in a storyboard format on paper.

It is a remarkably realistic portrayal of an antagonist. Curley does not set out to murder his wife, but these two students drew on Curley's prior actions in the story, such as him lashing out at Lennie, and applied his history of violent outbursts to this scenario. This required that they understand the characters and their motivations well. These two students in particular had a tendency not to complete other assignments in the class, so their performance on this project was particularly excellent compared to their usual work. That speaks to the impact and usefulness of allowing students choices in how they demonstrate their learning. Being able to use visual storytelling in this project increased their motivation to complete it.

The teacher should adequately prepare students for extension projects by completing activities before, during, and after they read the novel. For example, the students in this class participated in the following activities in the four weeks before they began the project:

Dialogue Writing: Students were given short paragraph descriptions of three scenarios that commonly occur in high schools (drama between two friends, an argument between two siblings, and an interaction with a crush). They had to write dialogue for those interactions that told the story only by what the characters said. It was written in dramatic format. At the beginning of the lesson, the teacher played a short audio clip from a popular film and the students noted how many things they learned from just listening to the words.

Figurative Language: Students completed a kinesthetic activity in which they were given a list of types of figurative language with short definitions. In groups, they had to find examples of these in a chapter of *Of Mice and Men*. They would write the examples on colored paper and then glue those to poster paper to make an image that was symbolic to the story (such as a mouse, deck of cards, rabbit, puppy, records, gun, etc.).

Descriptive Language: Students also completed an activity based on the shell game from George Hillocks's *Narrative Writing* (1997). Students, in small groups, were given four pieces of very similar fabrics. They had to write descriptions of each on separate note cards that were detailed enough that someone else could accurately match the description to the fabric. They took a photo of the correct match on their phones, then mixed everything up and traded with another group, who then attempted to match the fabric and description. If the other group matched everything correctly, then they knew they had written good descriptions.

Theme Statements: Students took notes over theme for less than ten minutes, practiced using gradual release and a popular children's film, and then had to write a thematic statement paragraph using two pieces of evidence from the text.

Foldable Character Analysis: This activity was based on "Words They Say" and "Words Said About Them" in Jennifer Serravallo's *Reading Strategies Book* (2015). The students were given a short review of connotation and denotation. They were placed in small groups and randomly assigned a character from *Of Mice and Men*. Each group folded a paper into three even rectangles and labeled the boxes: "Group Information," "Words Said About Them," "Words They Say" (front side), and "Positive Connotation," "Negative Connotation," "Question: What does this tell you about your character?" (back side). As students read chapter 2 of the novel, they filled out the "Words Said About Them" and "Words They Say" portions. When they were done, they sorted those words on the back based on positive or negative connotation. To help the students, the teacher did the same activity on the board with the character Crooks.

Conclusion

How can extension and remix be applied to other texts? A teacher should start by asking what students need to learn. This technique was used in a narrative writing unit for ninth-grade students in a Midwestern state that bases its standards on the Common Core. ELA standards are often repetitive between grade levels with only minor changes. Some of the minor changes between eighth and ninth grade in this state include a focus on how complex characters affect the plot and theme, writing with multiple points of view, and writing a strong resolution. Those are common requirements across the country, and this project addressed all of them in depth.

Once teachers have determined what the students will need to know, they should choose a text. Often, due to resource limitations or budget concerns, there is very little choice in this matter. *Of Mice and Men* was used in this class because that was one of the texts the school had available for ninth-grade students. This technique can be applied to any grade-level appropriate text that has the ability to elicit strong reactions from readers. The activities that a teacher does to accompany the chosen novel should directly correlate to the requirements in the final extension or remix project.

The final consideration should be for the project parameters. A good extension or remix project will have some student autonomy and choice, but also very clear expectations, to avoid students feeling too lost. The appropriate mix of choice and specifications will vary depending on the students. However, the goal will not change. In many English classrooms, teachers have their students study beautifully crafted canonical texts in the hopes that students will learn to be better writers thereby. However, extension and remix actually challenge them to write like those great writers. When students are immersed in a well-crafted text and then asked to write something else, often much of the information gained from reading does not transfer over to their own writing. When they see their own writing as an extension of the "mentor" text, they have a direct model to work from and their writing is almost universally better, while still being their own work.

The power of extension and remix lies in the fact that students are given the opportunity to change the text. With this epitextual model, students can feel increased confidence in their writing because they are told, through the hidden curriculum, that they are worthy of writing something like one of those great canonical texts that are often placed on such high pedestals.

A well-crafted extension or remix project accepts that the students will make decisions about the text that are supported by evidence, but may not be the decision that the teacher would have made—and that this variety is a good thing. It is open-ended and allows students to write creatively. In fact, the disagreement that will occur between students over how a story should end or be changed is an excellent excuse for students to read their final products out loud, engage in civil discourse, and promote discussion that will naturally lead to even more literary analysis, just like in online fan-fiction communities.

Reflecting on Your Learning

In theory, any text can inspire the creation of extension texts, but in practice, some texts lend themselves more readily to such activities. Can you think of examples of texts that would be effective "starter" texts? Can you think of examples of texts that would be less effective? What are the differences in the characteristics of those two different groups of texts?

References

Anonymous State Department of Education. (2019). Anonymous report card. https://ksreportcard.ksde.org/demographics.aspx?org_no=D0500& bldg_no=8350&rptType=1

Curwood, J. (2013). Fan fiction, remix culture, and the Potter Games. In V. E. Frankel (ed.), *Teaching with Harry Potter* (pp. 81–92). Jefferson, NC: McFarland.

Hillocks, G. (1997). *Narrative writing: Learning a new model for teaching.* Portsmouth, NH: Heinemann.

Lee, H. (1960). *To kill a mockingbird.* Philadelphia: J. B. Lippincott.

McWilliams, J., Hickey, D. T., Hines, M. B., Conner, J. M., & Bishop, S. C. (2011). Using collaborative writing tools for literary analysis: Twitter, fan fiction and *The Crucible* in the secondary English classroom. *Journal of Media Literacy Education, 2*(3): 238–245.

Rosenblatt, L. (1978). *The reader, the text, the poem: The transactional theory of the literary work.* Carbondale: Southern Illinois University Press.

Serravallo, J. (2015). *The reading strategies book: Your everything guide to developing skilled readers.* Portsmouth, NH: Heinemann.

Steinbeck, J. (1937). *Of mice and men.* New York: Covici-Friede.

PART II

Epitext and Critical Thinking

CHAPTER 5

Laurie Halse Anderson's *Wintergirls* Epitexts

A Hard Book to Read but Worth Every Tear

James Blasingame

Laurie Halse Anderson's award-winning book, *Wintergirls* (2009), pulls back the curtain to reveal the secret thoughts of Lia, a young woman suffering the typical causes and effects of anorexia. Especially for readers who deeply identify with Lia, epitextual analysis of promotion and reception of the book may provide another point of entry into understanding Anderson's reasons for writing this book. Both before its release and in the outpouring of reviews later, epitexts about the novel provide a consistent message to potential readers: this book is a serious story about a tragic subject that the author took very much to heart, handling it with the utmost care and concern. Before the book was released, at the time of its launch, and over the years following, materials about the book have maintained this stance and tone. Potential readers should have no doubt that this is likely to be a hard read, albeit a meaningful one. Tweets, blogs, reviews, book trailers, and awards candidly discuss the quality of the work, the innovative handling of its first-person narrative, and the gravity of the topic, often comparing it to Anderson's critically acclaimed 1999 book *Speak,* which looked deeply into the damaged psyche of a sexual assault victim 18 years before #MeToo in 2017. Everything suggests a gut-wrenching book by a veteran author capable of examining heartbreaking life experiences rarely touched on in fiction.

First Indications: Dark and Devastating

Information prior to the book's release in March of 2009 left no doubt that this book would rise to the level of *Speak*, meeting its standard for both artistry and painful honesty. Pre-release reviews of the book describe the paradox of brilliantly written fiction depicting ruthless tragedy:

> ". . . In broken, symbolic and gut-wrenching prose, Lia narrates her hopeless story of the destructive behaviors that control her every action and thought . . ."
> —*Kirkus Reviews*, starred review (February 1, 2009)

> ". . . a devastating portrait of the extremes of self-deception. This is a brutal and poetic deconstruction of how one girl stealthily vanishes into the depths of anorexia . . ."
> —*Booklist*, starred review (Kraus, December 15, 2008)

> ". . . returning to psychological minefields akin to those explored in *Speak*, Anderson delivers a harrowing story overlaid with a trace of mysticism . . ."
> —*Publishers Weekly*, starred review (January 26, 2009)

While touring with *Chains* (2008) in the latter months of 2008, Anderson herself was not saying or posting much about *Wintergirls*; however, flashes of conversation suggested that this next book would have more in common with *Speak* than with any other Anderson book. On August 28, 2008, Anderson announced a *Wintergirls* release date of May 2009 in her blog, *Mad Woman in the Forest* (*Madwoman*), but she said readers could request an advance reader copy (ARC) if they won her book trailer contest "[i]f you are in the mood to be patient." On August 28, 2008, one *Madwoman* follower replied with an inquiry referring to a comment Anderson had made, possibly at an author appearance: "Any details on *Wintergirls*? It intrigues me that you called it your darkest book." Other followers must have been beside themselves—Anderson's "darkest book"?! *Speak* (sexual assault) and *Catalyst* (death of a parent) both dealt with dark issues, yet this book would be even darker?

Anderson replied the same day, candidly but with little in the way of concrete details:

> I'm still so close to the story I don't know how to describe it. My editor should have the flap [book jacket flap] copy written soon. I bet that will do a better job explaining things than I could at the moment.
>
> I can say that it's a YA, told from a girl's POV. And it's dark. Intense. A little scary, maybe. (Admin, 2008, August 28, paras. 2 & 3)

This teaser was a definite attention-grabber. Anderson had previously announced only the existence of *Wintergirls* with little or no accompanying information.

On November 21, 2008, Anderson flew directly from the National Book Awards ceremonies to the annual conventions of the National Council of Teachers of English (NCTE) and the Assembly on Literature for Adolescents of NCTE (ALAN) in San Antonio. On November 22 she was given the ALAN Award, an award for lifetime contribution to young adult literature. Two days later, as approximately 500 participants in the ALAN Workshop opened their Workshop box of complimentary books, they found ARCs of *Wintergirls*. This put the book in the hands of some of the most influential and media-active YA experts in the world (librarians, teachers, professors, scholars, publishers, agents, and authors) whose networks would soon buzz with comments on the book's content and quality. Returning to her blog on the final day of the ALAN Workshop, Anderson told her followers that the release date was now March 2009, instead of May, and promised to "blog about it soon. Like when my brain re-engages" (Anonymous, 2008, December 3).

Cover artwork unveilings are important steps in a publisher's marketing plan, and on November 25, 2008, *Madwoman* revealed the *Wintergirls* cover. The cover was largely taken up with a young woman's stoic face, partially obscured, composed primarily of shades of black and blue. The young woman's situation is unclear but definitely not good. She appears to be being looking through a window that is partially frosted over. Across the middle of the cover is the title "*wintergirls*" all in lower case. The largest thing on the cover is the author's name in all capital letters along with "NEW YORK TIMES BESTSELLING AUTHOR," smaller but in all capitals. The cover is intriguing but joyless in tone: not exactly alarming or sinister, but surely sad and indicative of a heart-breaking story.

> Book covers are essentially peritext, but act as epitext when the production history of a work is mapped through its editions. In what other ways can epitext become peritext?

The cover art for a book in its second edition/paperback reprintings is often nothing like the original, often taking a different approach to portraying a book's content in an attempt to better align the cover with the content. Not so with *Wintergirls*. Less than a year after its release in March 2009, the paperback edition came out with only one small change. In the February 2010 reprint edition from Penguin, wording was added at the top of cover saying, "You're not dead, but you're not alive. You're a wintergirl. . . ."

Readers' Revelations: Brilliant but Brutal

After that first cover reveal on *Madwoman* on November 25, and as the ARCs were feverishly digested by Anderson aficionados and/or ALAN Workshop participants, the reactions begin hitting the public and blogosphere. Two reactions appeared on *Madwoman* the very next day, November 26, 2008, from readers who had received ARCs at the ALAN Workshop. Both posts were complimentary of the book ("beyond brilliant"), and one, anonymously, made a comment that would be repeated over and over going forward: the story is heartbreaking but the book is one readers cannot put down.

> Anyhow, finished *Wintergirls* over Thanksgiving . . . OH MY GOD! That last scene in the motel, the parallelism w/ what happened to Cassie, the guilt, the slow withdrawal from life and pain . . . it was more than I could take but I couldn't stop reading. (Anonymous, December 3, 2008).

Anderson includes URLs for sites where three reviews of ARCs can be read, including a review from the United Kingdom's *The Bookbag* website (2008). An early blog post based on an ARC from renowned YA expert Julie Prince, in her blog on *LiveJournal* on December 2, 2008, centers on the voice:

> And a real girl is narrating! I mean, I *know* her! She's everygirl. Everygirl with big problems. Doesn't every girl have big problems? This book is written with heart. It has soul. It breathes. It lives on its own, thanks to the way you poured everything you had into it. I can't even begin to imagine how draining that process must have been.

In addition, Prince offers her own blurb of the book in response to a blog reader's request: "When Lia's ex-best-friend is found dead alone in a motel room, Lia must deal with the guilt of not answering her phone the 33 times her friend called the night she died . . . and anorexic cutters like Lia don't do guilt well."

By December 2008, the ARC reviews and comment postings were fast and furious, usually touting how authentic the voice feels, how accurately anorexia is depicted, and how deeply the story slips into readers' hearts and minds. This reply on *Madwoman* came from a bookstore employee in Houston:

> I just had to email you about Wintergirls; it still haunts me weeks after I've read it. I've never been close to anyone with an eating disorder, but after reading Lia's story, I feel like I am now.
>
> The weekend I read it, I had to read it in pieces because it was so intense, and my dear husband kept saying, "If it upsets you that much, just put it down!"
>
> But I couldn't. I felt I owed it to Lia to finish her story, no matter what happened.
>
> I'm already farming out ARCs to local teachers, librarians and teens.
>
> Lia will stay with me for a long time and I hope she will stay with other readers, too.
>
> Brava! (https://madwomanintheforest.com/2008/12/09/whats-my-name /#comments)

The trade journals were equally impressed with Anderson's unflinching examination of the topic. On January 26, 2009, *Publishers Weekly*, which would later place *Wintergirls* on its Best Books for 2009 list, offered a very positive critique, ending with, "As difficult as reading this novel can be, it is more difficult to put down." But the review is quite clear from the first sentence that this is not a happy story:

> Acute anorexia, self-mutilation, dysfunctional families and the death of a childhood friend—returning to psychological minefields akin to those explored in *Speak*, Anderson delivers a harrowing story overlaid with a trace of mysticism.

On January 21, 2009, a Facebook page devoted to *Wintergirls* first opened. It includes an iconic black-and-white picture of the author in a jeans jacket, backgrounded by a large tree with what appears to be an ancient heart carved into its bark that has scarred over and is healing shut. Many publicity pictures of Anderson can be found in cyberspace, but this one is the most somber. By April of 2020, that Facebook page had received 2,310 likes and 2,302 follows. It received 11 public posts before the book launched for public purchase, although references to ARCs and professional reviews pepper the comments. Readers who were able to get ARCs were meticulously careful not to accidentally post spoilers; nevertheless, they make clear that this book will make readers feel like the story is happening to them. Most posts were from fans unable to secure ARCs, and they refer to previous Anderson books as favorite reads, expressing their anticipation for another book just as good or better, as well as their envy for peers who did get ARCs.

One month prior to release, *School Library Journal* was one of the first sources to report on Anderson's innovative use of fonts, crossed-out words and phrases, italics, and white space to express the narrator's conflicted feelings and confused thoughts:

> As events play out, Lia's guilt, her need to be thin, and her fight for acceptance unravel in an almost poetic stream of consciousness in this startlingly crisp and pitch-perfect first-person narrative. The text is rich with words still legible but crossed out, the judicious use of italics, and tiny font-size refrains reflecting her distorted internal logic. (Edwards, 2009)

The phrase "distorted internal logic" suggests that this book has a new kind of unreliable narrator, one who is somehow aware of her psychosis but unable to resist it. By this ingenious means, Anderson underscores one of anorexia's scientifically measured attributes, *alexithymia*, a medical term used by psychologists for the inability to identify and communicate feelings, which has a statistically significant correlation to anorexia and bulimia nervosa (Nowakowski, McFarlane, & Cassin, 2013).

Has the use of social media such as Facebook, Twitter, and Goodreads by authors and others affected the success of a book or movie you like?

Anderson opened a Twitter account, @halseanderson, for the first time in January 2009 and soon thereafter began references to *Wintergirls*:

"One month til the WINTERGIRLS book tour. Already fretting about what to wear" (@halseanderson - 4:50 AM - 19 Feb 2009)

followed by

> "Early mention of Wintergirls in USA Today's Book Buzz: http://tinyurl.com/cw5l6g." (@halseanderson - 8:44 AM - 26 Feb 2009)

USA Today did indeed connect the dots between *Speak* and the soon-to-be-released *Wintergirls*.

> Speaking out: It's been a decade since Laurie Halse Anderson's novel *Speak*, about a teenage girl who refuses to talk after she is sexually assaulted. . . . A 10th anniversary edition hits stores on March 19 (Puffin, $11.99, paperback),

the same day Viking releases Anderson's next novel, *Wintergirls* ($17.99, ages 12 and up), about a teenage girl with an eating disorder. At a lunch this week in New York, Anderson, 47, said she's heard from many readers since *Speak* was published, some sharing their stories of battling anorexia and bulimia. "Don't say teenagers don't read, because they do," Anderson says. "I hope that they'll read *Wintergirls*, and if they're struggling with (an eating disorder), it will help them." (Minzesheimer, Thai, & Donahue, 2009, para. 2)

On March 5, 2019, the International Reading Association and National Council of Teachers of English collaboration ReadWriteThink released an interview with Anderson in Episode 12 of "Text Messages for Teen Readers," a podcast from young adult literature expert and ALAN officer Dr. Jennifer Buehler, in anticipation of *Wintergirls*. Buehler sets the context by listing the author's accomplishments, including receiving the Margaret A. Edwards Award for Lifetime Contribution to Young Adult Literature, and announcing the approaching ten-year anniversary of *Speak*. Buehler explains the sensitive and difficult subject matter of *Speak* (rape and harassment), the courage and importance of Anderson's tackling this subject matter, and the awards the book has won. Buehler gives a short plot summary before launching into an interview with Anderson.

The interview revolved around the necessity and power in addressing dark subjects in books for teens (all quotations in this paragraph refer to the podcast: Buehler, March 1, 2009). Anderson explained that she wrote *Wintergirls* because so many young women had revealed their struggles with eating disorders to her. Anderson explained that, like most women in the United States, she had struggled with eating issues and continues to hear those voices in her head saying, "'You're ugly, you're fat, you're stupid,' which corrodes your sense of self." She did not want to write this book because she knew it would be personal to her, and "when you're writing about a character, you become that character, and I didn't know if I was strong enough to go back into that pain." Emails and letters from girls who had read *Speak* or *Catalyst* or *Prom* would share their enthusiasm for those books and "usually in the third paragraph, say 'you know, I'm not doing so good.'" The email would often turn out to have been written under supervision from a rehabilitation clinic after the young woman had engaged in harmful behavior: "I think that I am hideous [fat], but you can see all my ribs."

> Consider how many types of epitext affect the success of a work, from the pre-production stage through its post-publication life.

> This is similar to points made by Toliver (chapter 6 of this book) on the usefulness of authorial epitext to enhance reader comprehension of a text.

Anderson explains that she felt a need to help and started talking to professionals in the field: "I learned that until the person who is trapped in the behavior/addiction chooses for themselves that they're ready to reach for help, there's nothing anyone can do." Lia was born to help people understand the nature of eating disorders and the path to recovery. The podcast ends with a poem from Anderson in which she echoes the emails she has received from thousands of teens who have suffered deeply because of rape, abuse, addiction, and eating disorders—emails asking for her help or thanking her for a book (*Speak*, *Catalyst*, etc.) that validated their lives and struggles.

On March 11, 2009, during the final week before the book's release, Penguin Teen posted a silent *Wintergirls* book trailer (https://www.youtube.com/watch?v=DIjyJ_tqedc) on YouTube. Against the book cover background, words flash on the screen one at a time, faster and faster, accelerating until they are a blur: "Must." "Not." "Eat." Then the words, "I swear to be the skinniest girl in school." appear as the face of the young woman from the book cover begins to fade in behind the text. "Skinnier than you." appears next as the young woman's face continues to fade in, not completely in focus. Next, "'As difficult as reading this book can be, it is even more difficult to put it down.'—Publishers Weekly starred review" appears for five seconds of the 47-second trailer, then fades out as the young woman's face fades into focus, her one visible eye closed. As the title *Wintergirls* appears in large letters, the young woman's closed eye opens and "From Laurie Halse Anderson, the author of *Speak* On Sale March 19, 2009" fades in at the bottom of the screen and remains for the final 12 seconds. Again, the connection to *Speak* is made for potential readers. Between *Speak* and *Wintergirls* Anderson published 20 other works of fiction, but *Speak* is the one that publicists, marketers, and the author keep referring to.

Replies on YouTube in 2009 repeated the refrain that had been established. *Wintergirls* is a hard but rewarding read that resembles *Speak*: "this book was amazing! sad but such a great story truly remarkable ♥." "both Speak and Wintergirls made me cry . . . extremely wonderful and emotional books. <3 them both." "I loved this book so much. I could never put it down. You really felt like you were in Lia's position, and I highly recommend it."

The Conversation Begins: Author, Reader, Anorexic

On March 19, 2009, Penguin released *Wintergirls* for sale at bookstores and online around the world. Epitexts from this point forward remain consistent with those from prerelease. The message is the same: this is a serious book, artfully written in an innovative format by an author who has an intense connection to the book's issue. It is a difficult, meaningful, deeply moving read. The publisher, Viking/Penguin, describes the book in much the same way amateur and professional reviewers do: "In her most emotionally wrenching, lyrically written book since the multiple-award-winning *Speak*, Laurie Halse Anderson explores Lia's descent into the powerful vortex of anorexia, and her painful path toward recovery, and her desperate attempts to hold on to the most important thing of all: hope." (Penguin Random House, n.d., para. 1)

Tweets for the next few months announced *Wintergirls*' debut on the New York Times Bestseller list, where it remained each week for a long time. A year later, Anderson tweeted "Just found out that the WINTER-GIRLS paperback will be on the New York Times list 4/18. Thank you booksellers!!! #indiebound #indielove." Anderson also tweeted about giving her mother the book and what airport bookstores she had seen the book in while on tour.

As the months went by, Anderson tweeted about the avalanche of awards the book received. In addition, she alerted followers every time the book appeared in a new country and/or a new language; for example: "Just found out that WINTERGIRLS is going to be translated into both Simplified and Complex Chinese. Must ponder this. #smallworld." (@halseanderson 4:57 PM - 8 Dec 2010) and "Am signing contracts for Lithuanian version of WINTERGIRLS" (@halseanderson 10:05 AM - 14 Nov 2011). At times she revealed her personal experience writing the book: "The writing process of WINTERGIRLS was intense. Many, many tears" (@halseanderson 12:56 PM - 3 Jun 2011). Anderson often retweets messages on self-care for people in the eating disorder struggle at the moment, such as "Talk to your therapist. Have a support team. Slip ups are not failure. Recovery is worth it. Keep going. Life is waiting" from @AnnieZomaya (@halseanderson 1:09 PM - 20 Jul 2015).

Anderson's *Wintergirls* book tour cut a whirlwind swath across the United States, touching down at iconic bookstores across the country and then flying on. On March 28, 2009, the tour landed in Tempe, Arizona, at the legendary Changing Hands Bookstore, the *Publishers Weekly* 2007 Bookseller of the Year. The majority of the audience members were young women, who were visibly pleased to be face-to-face with one of their favorite authors. Despite Anderson's gregarious personality and the heartfelt devotion of these fans, the event was somber. The author opened with some alarming statistics from the previous year:

- Anorexia is the third most common chronic illness among adolescents

- 95% of those who have eating disorders are between the ages of 12 and 25

- 50% of girls between the ages of 11 and 13 see themselves as overweight

- 80% of 13-year-olds have attempted to lose weight

- Eating disorder statistics are similar in the United States for young women of all ethnic groups

- 20% of people suffering from anorexia will prematurely die from complications related to their eating disorder, including suicide and heart problems

- Eating disorders have the highest mortality rate of any mental illness (Anderson, March 28, 2009)

At the Changing Hands appearance, Anderson explained the homework she did to ensure the book's accuracy. She looked up statistics, read research literature, and spoke with professionals. She pointed out that the great majority of teens with eating disorders will never receive treatment, and the majority of those who do will not get anywhere near the level and length of treatment required for recovery because of the cost in relation to health insurance policy coverage limits. She told us there is no simple remedy, and that there are multiple causes for the illness, including genetic predisposition, cultural pressures, and life events. Effective solutions require a complete program addressing all aspects of the problem, but the first step comes in identifying the issue. A variety of forms of support from a variety of people in the person's life are needed, but until the person admits something is wrong, anorexia/bulimia nervosa cannot be treated successfully.

As the first year post-release continued, *Madwoman* followers began referring to the emotional release they felt at the book's ending, usually manifesting in some form of crying. At the same time, the paradox continued of how Anderson's story is both horrible and wonderful at the same time:

> Wintergirls is brilliant. I just finished it Wednesday. I found the internal dialogue to be very realistic while your writing was creative in expressing it.

I knew it was going to be dark but I never expected the depth with the haunt-ings. I think you did a really great job showing the horrors of such a real life problem in the world. Thank you for doing that. I would like to someday be able to teach this novel in my classroom as a literature circle book. This subject needs to be spoken about more especially in the schools.

Post-release readers often used the word "amazing," and many also expressed hopes for a movie. A few months after the release, *Win-tergirls'* Facebook posts began to link to youth reviews and youth-created playlists to match the story's mood. At a year out, posts started to ask for other similar books and to express the impact of the book: "It really changed my point of view. I mean it! Great book!!" As time went by and the novel was no longer new, the posts lengthened and often discussed the book's long-term effect on readers' perspectives on eating disorders. Three years out, the posts started to come from other countries, sometimes in languages other than English. The public posts ended in 2013.

Public Conclusions: Nothing Hard Is Easy/ *Wintergirls* Provides Much Needed Help

Awards are a prime source of marketing material for successful books, underscoring a book's value as attested to by the award giver. *Wintergirls* won scores of awards large and small, including the Chicago Tribune Award for Top Ten Influential Books of the Decade. It also made the AARP Top 20 Books for Summer Reading for Students, which recom-mends that retirees should read it, too (O'Connor, 2013). It won the 2010 American Library Association Best Books for Young Adults Award, as well as awards from Arizona, Colorado, Georgia, Iowa, New Hamp-shire, Rhode Island, and Tennessee.

Wintergirls took up residence on Goodreads, including a Question and Answer account where Anderson answered 183 questions from 2009 to 2019. Popular questions dealt with why she wrote the book, the impact on her psyche as she dealt with such a toxic topic, and how she deals with backlash for writing about difficult subjects:

Q: What inspired you to write a story like *Wintergirls*? It's one of my favorite books of all time!

A: Hearing from readers who were struggling with eating disorders made me want to write about their battle. Eating disorders have the highest fatality rate of any mental illness. I wanted to tell a story that would show people how devastating they are.

Q: Was it emotionally challenging for you to write books like *Speak* and *Wintergirls*?

A: During the writing process I had to practice regular self-care, making sure I had plenty of time away [from] the stories, and getting outside to clear my head.

Q: I haven't read anything of yours in months, but I often think about your characters, mainly Hayley and Ash. My question is this: is it scary to publish books about teens who are so brutally (but truthfully) real? It's hard to accept the things that highschoolers go through, from substance abuse to broken families, but you do so with grace and apparently without fear. Do you receive a lot of backlash for these things?

A: I've received plenty of backlash, but I know that any pain it might cause me doesn't come close to the pain suffered by teens who are dealing with these issues.

The criticism I've gotten for writing honestly about sexual violence, bullying, mental health, eating disorders, and the horrific reality of American slavery comes from adults who do not know how to talk about these things to their kids. Rather than confront their own fear and ignorance, they lash out at me (and other authors). I understand their pain. It proves that there is an enormous need for books like mine.

Maybe if we keep writing books about these things and promote conversations about the harsh realities of our world, we can help a generation learn how to handle the truth and grow up in strength and wisdom. (https://www.goodreads.com/author/10003.Laurie_Halse _Anderson/questions)

Wintergirls received 8,688 Goodreads reviews and 101,662 ratings with an average of four out of five stars. Reviewers seem to fall into one of two camps. The majority find it "brilliant," "amazing," "a unique voice . . . with a style that is like a puzzle and a poem, at once," "Lia's voice is the voice of an anorexic to a 't'; The anger, the bitterness, the resentment, the cold-hearted carelessness was so true, it's almost frightening," and "[Laurie Halse Anderson] has a way of explaining inner thoughts in beautiful and heart-breaking words and phrases, and while the language is poetic it doesn't drown the actual story." A few Goodreads reviewers found the unusual writing style using cross-outs and changes in font size distracting, but most reviewers found this an innovative way of expressing a difficult mental illness (see the definition of "alexithymia" earlier in this chapter).

The second camp of reviewers is disturbed by the book. In the very next month after the book comes out, one reviewer expressed concern that Anderson's story will make the problem worse for readers who suffer from anorexia: "for those with disordered eating, I think it would be very triggering. So really, I wouldn't recommend *Wintergirls* to anyone." One reviewer captured what most naysayers contend:

> While this book doesn't outwardly glorify eating disorders, the majority of the book is basically a triggering how-to manual, while only a small minority of the book is heartfelt recovery (if you can even call it that?). I hope I'm wording my point clearly; if not, I will elaborate in a more thorough review to come.

> Also, if you've read this book and find it relatable and/or helpful, hats off to you. But seriously, if you really do suffer from a severe eating disorder like I do, don't go near this book with a ten foot long pole. It isn't worth the risk or the time (IN MY OPINION.)

This begs the question of how this book affects young people with eating disorders. Should they read it or not? Is it a how-to manual for self-harm, or a life preserver thrown to drowning teens? Many of the reviewers claimed to suffer from eating disorders like the protagonist, Lia, and to be fair, most typically, those who claimed to find themselves in this book wrote reviews like this one:

> when i first picked up wintergirls, i was wading quickly into the deep end of an eating disorder without even realising it. this book marked the first point in time that i came to realise that i was sick. while i still struggle with my ED, this book was an extreme eye-opener for me. it made me want to recover, and i'm more grateful for that than i can put into words.

"It made me want to recover." No reader's testimonial better sums up what the majority of epitexts communicated. Video book trailers, tweets, professional and amateur reviews, blurbs, awards, interviews, blogs, live appearances, the book cover, and podcasts all worked together to tell readers (both prior to reading and while they were processing the actual text) something very much the same: This book is not entertainment, but it is artful. This book is about a deadly disease that deserves an honest and determined assault by one of the best young adult fiction writers of our time. In the words of Anderson herself, in a message tweeted in the years after *Wintergirls* was no longer an unknown commodity but among the most awarded books in YA book history: "People said #wintergirls was too scary and intense. Nope. It's a sad reflection of the ED nightmare too many kids are trapped in. #yalitchat." (@halseanderson 4:57 AM - 9 Sep 2013).

Moving from Theory to Practice

Epitexts might be considered the proverbial two-thirds of the iceberg not visible to the eye but undeniably keeping the visible third floating above the surface. Investigating the epitexts lying beneath *Wintergirls* may give students remarkable insight into the author's intention and the context within which the book was written. Epitextual analysis is likely to be most meaningful and intrinsically motivated by individual readers with whom the book resonated personally, rather than attempting the analysis with a whole class, including individuals with little personal connection to eating issues.

> What other authors do you follow in social media and digital spaces? How might you incorporate their work outside of their main texts to inform students' comprehension and engagement to the main texts?

Readers love making personal connections to their favorite authors, and Laurie Halse Anderson has been one of the most popular authors of books for young adults since *Speak* hit bookstore shelves in 1999. Fans attend her book launches in throngs, and her blog posts at Mad Woman in the Forest get thousands of comments. Most often, readers quickly communicate how their personal lived experience intersects with a book, and give a deeply felt thank-you for how the book validates their feelings and even their lives. By examining epitexts of *Wintergirls,* readers might come to understand more about themselves, the author, and the story.

Big Ideas

1. Important books can be hard to read, eliciting an emotional and even disturbing response, but this does not necessarily mean they are not worth the emotional difficulty.

2. Literature plays an important role in making sense of life, both for the reader and for the author.

3. Some reading experiences benefit from prereading orientation to their content.

4. Understanding an author's intent can help the reader to understand the overall context of the book and its message.

Essential Questions

1. How do publishers and authors typically create and use epitexts, and for what purpose?

2. Why might a book's epitexts follow a different path than the typical commercial promotion?

3. How have a particular book's epitexts affected your experience with that book?

4. In *Wintergirls*, what was Laurie Halse Anderson saying about the nature of eating disorders, and how did epitexts surrounding the book bear witness to this?

Activities

Teachers might assign all of these activities or choose from among them.

1. Prereading:

   Copy and paste references to *Wintergirls* in Anderson's blog Mad Woman in the Forest from 2008–2010 into a chronological chart. Be sure to include the date and who wrote the reference (e.g., Anderson, a reader, a teacher, a librarian, a professional reviewer, a fellow author). Write a journal entry (about 500 words) detailing your expectations for the experience of reading this book based on this chart. How do you think you will change as a result of reading *Wintergirls*? How do you think your understanding of eating disorders will change/grow?

2. During reading:

   Read through Common Sense Media's online resources about *Wintergirls* (https://www.commonsensemedia.org/book-reviews/winter girls) after choosing an identity to assume from the following: (1) a young reader, (2) a young reader who has experience with body image issues involving friends or self, (3) a young reader who has experience with eating issues involving friends or self, (4) a parent who may have a child with a body image or eating issues, (5) a teacher, or (6) a librarian. Next, staying in your role, write one paragraph recommending that your school or child's school does or does not purchase this book for the library. Explain what benefits this will provide or what damage you think it might do.

3. Postreading

   After reading *Wintergirls*, read through this chapter to familiarize yourself with the epitexts that surrounded this book. Now, pretend you are Laurie Halse Anderson and write a letter to the marketing division at Viking (now Penguin Random House) in which you/she recommend the following:

a. Which <u>one</u> of the commercial reviews (Kirkus, *Booklist*, or *Publisher's Weekly*) to use in marketing and what words and phrases from that review will be most helpful to prospective readers.

b. Which <u>two</u> of the seven statistical facts on eating disorders to include in an advertisement for *Wintergirls* to be placed in the *Journal of Adolescent and Adult Literacy*, and explain how these two complement each other.

c. Find one Goodreads review that describes *Wintergirls* as a harmful book for teens and list two of its arguments. For each point, write one paragraph in which you agree or disagree and explain why.

Reflecting on Your Learning

What forms of epitext have you generated in response to a work? What types of epitext have been most useful to you in deciding whether to engage with a work or not? Does epitext that serves a promotional function also work to increase comprehension of a work?

References

Admin. (2008, August 28). Me as Robinson Crusoe. [Blog post]. https://madwomanintheforest.com/2008/08/27/me-as-robinson-crusoe

Anderson, L. H. (1999). *Speak*. Harrisonburg, VA: R. R. Donnelly & Sons.

Anderson, L. H. (2008). *Chains*. New York: Bloomsbury.

Anderson, L. H. (2008, August 28). Book trailer contest revision. [Blog post]. https://madwomanintheforest.com/2008/08/26/book-trailer-contest-revision

Anderson, L. H. (2008, August 28). Me as Robinson Crusoe. [Blog post]. https://madwomanintheforest.com/2008/08/27/me-as-robinson-crusoe

Anderson, L. H. (2009). *Wintergirls*. New York: Viking.

Anderson, L. H. (2009, March 28). *Wintergirls*. Lecture at Changing Hands Bookstore, Tempe, AZ.

Anderson, L. H. (2010). *Wintergirls*. New York: Penguin.

Anonymous. (2008, August 28). Me as Robinson Crusoe. [Blog post] *Mad Woman in the Forest*. https://madwomanintheforest.com/2008/08/27/me-as-robinson-crusoe

Anonymous. (2008, December 3). NCTE ALAN fun and festivities. [Blog post]. https://madwomanintheforest.com/2008/11/25/nctealan-fun-festivities/#comments

Autumnash. (2009, April 3). Flowers from home. [Blog post]. *Mad Woman in the Forest*. https://madwomanintheforest.com/2009/04/01/flowers-from-home

Bibliopinions. (2008, December 10). What's my name. [Blog post]. https://madwomanintheforest.com/2008/12/09/whats-my-name/#commentsthe

Bookbag, The. (2008, November 24). *Wintergirls* by Laurie Halse Anderson. [Review of the book *Wintergirls*, by Laurie Halse Anderson]. *The Book Bag*. http://www.thebookbag.co.uk/reviews/index.php?title =Wintergirls_by_Laurie_Halse_Anderson

Buehler, J. (Host). (2009, March 1). A conversation with Laurie Halse Anderson [Audio podcast episode 12]. In *ReadWriteThink*. NCTE/ILA. http://www.readwritethink.org/parent-afterschool-resources/podcast -episodes/conversation-with-laurie-halse-30330.html

Edwards, C. A. (2009). [Review of *Wintergirls*, by L. H. Anderson]. *School Library Journal, 55*(2): 96.

Jenlyn_b. (2008, November 26). NCTE ALAN fun and festivities. [Blog post]. https://madwomanintheforest.com/2008/11/25/nctealan-fun-festivities /#comments

Kirkus Reviews. (2009, February 1). Wintergirls. [Review of *Wintergirls*, by L. H. Anderson]. *Kirkus Reviews*. https://www.kirkusreviews.com /book-reviews/laurie-halse-anderson/wintergirls

Kraus, D. (2008, December 15). Wintergirls. [Review of *Wintergirls*]. *Booklist Online*. http://alaboldev.coetruman.com/Wintergirls/pid=3201361 ?AspxAutoDetectCookieSupport=1

Minzesheimer, B., Thai, K., & Donahue, D. (2009, February 27). Book buzz. *USA TODAY*. https://usatoday30.usatoday.com/life/books/news/2009 -02-25-book-buzz_N.htm#

Nowakowski, M. E., McFarlane, T., & Cassin, S. (2013). Alexithymia and eating disorders: A critical review of the literature. *Journal of Eating Disorders, 1*(21). https://doi.org/10.1186/2050-2974-1-21

O'Connor, A. (2013, June 20). High school summer reading lists for 2013: 20 books today's students are diving into—and why you may want to read them, too. *AARP Entertainment Books*. https://www.aarp.org /entertainment/books/info-06-2013/books-to-read-this-summer.html

Penguin Random House. (n.d.). About *Wintergirls*. https://www.penguinrandom house.com/books/300980/wintergirls-by-laurie-halse-anderson

Prince, J. (2008, December 2). An open letter to Laurie Halse Anderson. *Live-Journal*. https://jmprince.livejournal.com/88893.html

Publishers Weekly. (2009, January 26). Wintergirls. [Review of *Wintergirls* by L. H. Anderson]. https://www.publishersweekly.com/978-0-670-01110-0

Critically Analyzing Black Female YA Speculative Fiction Alongside Author-Produced Epitext

S. R. Toliver

I hoped that the song would give the reader a
notion of some of the sensibility behind many creoles.
But I may have been too subtle.

—Nalo Hopkinson

In an interview (Hopkinson & Nelson, 2002), Alondra Nelson asked Jamaican-born speculative fiction author, Nalo Hopkinson, about her intention behind including a poem at the beginning of her novel *Midnight Robber*. In response, Hopkinson asserted that she hated telling people that she planned for them to respond in particular ways to the works that she had written. She also acknowledged her amusement in seeing the various ways that readers interpreted her fiction writing. However, she confessed that although she did not want to tell readers what to think, she wanted the poem to give readers more information about creole sensibilities. In fact, she admitted that she was slowly realizing that people did not have adequate cultural and historical knowledge to fully understand some of the information in her texts, and she claimed that "those readers won't know that the resulting creoles are part enforced compliance, part defiance, and a whole lot of creativity" (p. 102). Essentially, although Hopkinson did not want to force her authorial intent onto the reader, she still implied that some readers would need certain knowledge to fully understand the perspective from which she was writing.

> This is one example of how epitext can be used to improve comprehension of a work.

Although Hopkinson condemned the need to explain the purpose behind specific elements of her texts, contemporary Black female speculative fiction writers have been more willing to discuss certain themes embedded within their novels. In 2018, four Black female authors—Dhonielle Clayton, Tomi Adeyemi, Justina Ireland, and L. L. McKinney—published young adult speculative fiction novels with Black female protagonists. Each of the novels is highly acclaimed as shown on Goodreads and Amazon, and within these novels, each author has discussed social justice issues related to beauty standards, racism, and representation. However, instead of being subtle, like Hopkinson, each of the authors has used their websites, Twitter pages, radio and online interviews, and podcasts to ensure that readers, if they choose, can better understand the underlying social justice metaphors in their speculative worlds.

Statement of Issues to Be Considered

In using external media to help readers understand the sociopolitical influences that affect the narratives, Black female speculative fiction authors are granting readers another way to access critical information that would enhance the reading of the text. They are ensuring that even if readers do not have adequate cultural and historical knowledge to fully understand the underlying metaphors within the text, they still have a viable pathway to understanding by using the author's words as their guide. The use of material outside of the text by these authors presents a need to broaden beliefs about reading that relegate response to individual influences. In particular, these authors present the need to question how information outside of the text can influence a reader's response. Thus, the purpose of this chapter is to explore how a proliferation of epitext might complicate early conceptions of reader response theory. Specifically, this chapter asks how reading a text alongside the author's epitext can provide a method for enhancing reader responses and highlighting Black women authors' voices, concerns, and critiques.

Reader Response and Epitextual Theory

Reader response is a theory of reading that situates the reader as an active participant in the reading event. It opposes the formalist idea that the text contains all meaning and readers must extract meaning from the text. Instead, researchers who subscribe to this theory believe that readers create the meaning of the text through their own, different interpretations. Several reader-response scholars exclude the author's attempts at influencing reader response. For example, Iser (1972) stated that authors embed certain openings and silences in the text to allow readers to "fill in the gaps" using their imaginations, but he mocked authors who explicitly told readers what to think. Rosenblatt (1978) argued that "once the creative activity of the author has ended, what remains for others . . . is the text" (p. 15). Her claim suggests that once a text is written, the author is removed from the reading event, leaving behind only the symbols bound within the book. Although the author is mentioned by various reader-response theorists, discussions about the ways in which authors use various platforms to influence reader response have been understudied.

To broaden the scope and better situate authors' attempts at influencing aspects of a reader's response, it is essential to look toward epitextual theory. The epitext is a fluctuating threshold, a zone of transition or transaction on the fringe of a text that can "control one's whole reading of a text" (Genette, 1997, p. 2). Epitextual elements can communicate information, intention, interpretation, advice, or commands, and they function as supplementary discourses that are subordinate to the text (Genette, 1997). The combination of these materials, though, provides "the world at large the possibility of either stepping inside or turning back" (p. 2). That is, before people read a book, they may see a Goodreads review, a video book trailer, an author interview, or even an author's Twitter thread. This may influence their reading of the text, if they choose to read the book at all. Essentially, the epitext includes various aspects of a literary work that exist outside of the bounded story, and each of these elements can influence a reader's response.

> Compare this to Mackey's discussion in Chapter Eight, and consider the experience of being a "knowing" audience for a work.

It is important to note, however, that an expansion of reader response to include scholarship about the epitext does not assume the reader will automatically agree with the author's commentary. In fact, Genette (1997) advised that the presence of epitext does not ensure that a reader will take the time to engage with it. Yet, he also asserted that although it is not essential for people to know the information provided in the epitext, people who do know the information will respond to a text differently. Ultimately, both reader response and epitextual theory center on the ways in which readers make meaning of text. However, where reader response tends to highlight the story, epitextual theory expands response to include myriad influences unbound by the book. Moreover, where reader response often dismisses the author's intentions, epitextual theory focalizes how authors and their publishers use epitext to add important data to influence the reader's response. Thus, it is essential to connect the two theories in an effort to expand how reader-response scholarship is situated in the 21st century, where readers and authors are more connected than in previous years.

Review of Relevant Literature

Several theorists have noted the influence of peritext on student reading, but few have considered the influence or possible influence of the epitext. For example, Leavenworth (2015) studied a fan-fiction author's use of filing options, author's notes, and conversations with readers and found that external information can be used to ensure that readers know how to read a text. Additionally, Murray (2012) examined how the commercial decisions of a comic book company (including the creation of a major motion picture and the design of a mobile phone app), altered traditional comic consumption and created a communication pathway between creator and consumer. Although these scholars have focused on how the epitext has influenced reader response, scholarship that connects reader response and the epitext are minimal.

Still, one children's literature scholar, Rudine Sims Bishop (2007), noted the following in her discussion of children's books written by Black authors:

> African American children's books also often reflect or are influenced by the life experiences of their creators . . . the creators of African American children's literature all share the experience of being members of a society in which race matters a great deal more than it should . . . this eccentricity, this uneasy ideological difference, shapes the lenses through which Black authors and illustrators of children's books view their work and their worlds. (Introduction, pp. xi–xii)

In this excerpt, Bishop suggests that the identities and cultural experiences of Black authors influence the material present within their work.

She also insinuates that race and the troubled structures of society influence the writings of Black authors. Thus, Bishop's ideas imply that the Black female authors of these texts might feature embedded messages with culturally specific content that some readers may not understand.

The possible cultural influences of the text are even more poignant in speculative fiction because speculative authors often manipulate textual metaphors in an effort to influence readers' prior suppositions. When Nalo Hopkinson (Hopkinson & Nelson, 2002) was asked about the extrapolative differences between speculative fiction and realistic fiction, she stated:

> in fantastical fiction, I can directly manipulate the metaphorical structure of the story . . . one of the things I can do is to intervene in the readers' assumptions by creating a world in which standards are different. Or I can blatantly show what values the characters in the story are trying to live out by making them actual, by exaggerating them into the realm of the fantastical, so that the consequences conversely become so real that they are tangible. (p. 101)

Essentially, speculative fiction is a way to influence readers by creating worlds that are greatly different from the modern world, while also including commentary on the real world. Authors within the genre are not bound by the limitations of realism, and thus are able to create new metaphors and present social justice issues and solutions in nuanced ways. Therefore, it is essential to discuss the epitext created by Black female speculative fiction authors to better understand how they embed Black cultural experiences into narratives that are unbound by the restrictions of reality.

Context

Although various reader-response theorists argue that readers come to a text with a range of knowledge that influences how they will read the work, the author's creation of epitextual features assumes that some of the readers will not have the knowledge necessary to understand a major aspect of the work, especially if that is culturally specific knowledge. Additionally, although many reader-response theorists exclude the author as an important influence in the reader's interpretation, ignoring the epitext created by these authors could cause readers to miss a highly pertinent cultural aspect of the text, one that is centered in Black authorial traditions. With this in mind, it is essential to read the author's epitext alongside the text as a way to assist all readers in understanding the larger metaphors that underlie the narrative. Of course, the epitext will not provide the reader with a designated response, but it can provide another entry point through which readers can access critical information rooted within the narrative.

I am a Black female scholar who studies representations of and responses to people of color in speculative texts, with a specific focus on representations by, for, and about Black women and girls. The following section contains my text analysis of *The Belles* by Dhonielle Clayton (2018a) and *Children of Blood and Bone* by Tomi Adeyemi (2018), two speculative fiction books written by Black female authors. I do not give a complete overview of each text. Instead, the epitext is used as a means to connect a modern social justice issue to the text. In this way, my analysis will provide a practical example of supporting the reading of a text using the information given in each author's epitext.

Application of Approach

On her website, Dhonielle Clayton notes that her inspiration for *The Belles* (Clayton, 2018a) stemmed from her irritation over the commodification of women's body parts (Clayton, 2018b). Information from her website was corroborated in interviews, where she addressed society's focus on beauty as a major part of her book. In one interview (Jarema, 2018), she said she "was surprised by how many people are deeply dissatisfied by the body they have, and if given the chance to change it radically and magically, how many would jump at the opportunity" (para. 6). She also stated that she published the novel at the right time "because [US society is] at an interesting precipice in all industries about the role of women, their looks and sexuality, and how that interacts with misogyny and rape culture" (para. 14). Thus, Clayton uses epitext to discuss the ways in which society privileges certain aspects of beauty, as well as the various methods that people will use to obtain certain levels of attractiveness.

The hegemonic norms of beauty are shown throughout the text. *The Belles* is a novel set in the kingdom of Orléans, where people are born red-eyed and grey-skinned. That is, most people are considered aesthetically ugly in terms of dominant standards of beauty. Belles, who are young women with the power of beauty in their blood, can change the appearance of the citizens of Orléans and make them "beautiful." They are able to alter the residents' hair, eye, and skin color and change the shape and size of someone's body. They are also able to change someone's disposition, eliminating a person's unwanted personality traits. The main character, Camellia, is one of these Belles, and she is known for her ability to completely alter someone's physical body to make them beautiful.

The norms of beauty are regulated in the society by the Beauty Minister, a person who creates a set of laws that regulate the definition of beauty. Some laws, such as "Any bone restructuring or manipulation meant to deeply alter the shape of one's body or face is prohibited" and "Noses shall not be so slender as to impede the natural act of breathing" (p. 36) are created to ensure that people maintain some of their natural body structures. However, other laws, such as "no man shall be taller than the sitting king" and "fingers and toes shall remain at a ten-digit count so as to preserve the goddess of beauty's favorite number" (p. 36), are steeped in class and ability privilege that situates the norm of beauty as an arbitrary facet of the community that is made real by the laws of society.

Clayton crafts a society that hyperbolically reflects the unrealistic and often unobtainable standards of beauty in the modern world. By situating beauty as painful, expensive, and subjective based on the whims of the dominant society, Clayton highlights how contemporary society arbitrarily assigns beauty to certain members of society, causing many young people to hate the way they look. In the epitext, she discusses her personal connection to the standards of beauty, tying her personal narrative to the fictional story in her novel. She also outlines the various ways in which beauty culture in the United States has resulted in the oppression of women and femmes. The text and the epitext complement each other, highlighting a social issue that surrounds the sexualization and confinement of women's bodies.

Similar to Clayton, Tomi Adeyemi engaged in numerous interviews to assist readers in understanding the ideas behind her book. For example, in one interview (Young, 2018), she noted that her use of the word "maggot" was similar to a slur used against Black people. In another interview (Jones, 2018), she stated that the influx of videos presenting the brutality of the police force toward Black people caused an increase of fear. Specifically, she said, "But then it started coming from the police, so it went from fearing civilians to being terrified by the cops" (para. 15). Further, she mentioned that she "wanted to make that commentary, because we don't just worry about being killed by the cops—we worry about being raped by the cops. And that's part of oppression and the destructive power structure" (para. 27). In other words, Adeyemi's interviews not only address the racism and fear of police brutality experienced by Black people in the United States, but they also highlight the institutional violence that results in the murder and oppression of Black persons. These interviews highlight specific social justice concerns over police brutality, and they further highlight the message Adeyemi embeds within the story.

In her novel, *Children of Blood and Bone* (Adeyemi, 2018), Adeyemi tells the tale of Zelie, Amari, and Tzain as they travel to restore magic to the land of Orisha after it is forcefully destroyed by an evil dictator. The authoritarian king, Saran, killed all magical adults in the land, leaving their children, Diviners, to fend for themselves or be taken care of by nonmagical parents and relatives. Often referred to as "maggots," Diviners are heavily taxed merely for existing, and if they cannot pay the increasing fines, they are enslaved to work off their debt. To ensure that Diviners follow the rules, the king sends his guard, a military group that surveils all of Orisha and engages in brutal behaviors. They kill, rape, and maim Diviners at will, and they are praised for their actions, as they ensure the subjugation and death of the marginalized.

The brutality of the royal guard is shown when Zelie, Amari, and Tzain find an oasis for Diviners, a secluded area where Diviners fled in an attempt to avoid the king's persecution. The leader of this area is Zulaikha, a 13-year-old Diviner who led the other children to the forest after a royal raid occurred in their village. Zulaikha is a peaceful leader, and she protects all of the Diviners in the area, but she is not ignorant of the viciousness of the king and his royal guard. When sentries surround the village, she knows that they have the ability and strength to kill all the Diviners. Thus, to initiate goodwill, Zulaikha attempts to talk with the guards; however, her endeavor is quashed, as she is murdered before she gets the chance to speak.

The police state of Orisha presents a strong correlation with the current state of government surveillance and police brutality in the United States. Specifically, through her epitext Adeyemi tells readers that her novel, although based in the fantasy realm of Orisha, stems from the state-sanctioned violence and murder of Black children in the U.S. She implies that this violence was an underlying impetus for her creation of certain characters and the world in which they live. She announces in multiple spaces that the innocent Black children murdered by police were with her as she put the words on the page.

Ultimately, these authors are not providing explicit instructions about how to read their books, nor are they focused on taking away a reader's individual interpretation of the text. Instead, they specifically focus on an element of the story that may be too subtle for all readers to comprehend. They outline the connections between social justice issues in the modern world and the metaphoric representation of those issues in the speculative fiction worlds they create. Through the epitext, the authors presented in this analysis are attempting to fill in the gaps of interpretation by ensuring that readers see part of their authorial vision.

They are attempting to eliminate author silences by going on book tours, tweeting, speaking to various journalists, and engaging with a vast audience at conferences and in schools. They see importance in their themes that focalize social justice issues, and they want to share this with their readers.

> What function is author epitext that provides background or fills in gaps in the text fulfilling?

Theory to Practice

Black writers who write speculative fiction have stories to tell that differ from traditional conceptions of speculative authorship, as their work has historically been imbued with cultural commentary that connects to the lived realities of Black people (Dery, 1994). Because readers may have different realities, the cultural aspects included within such novels may not be realized or recognized by all readers, and the metaphors and cultural commentary they include may not be understood by those who do not share the same experiential background. So, as the authors include commentary about social justice issues that are prevalent in the world and greatly affect Black people, further explanation may be necessary. Using the author's epitext could ensure that all readers understand the larger themes embedded within the work.

However, because the epitext is supplementary, there is no guarantee that a reader will actually engage with it. Readers may never search online for the author's website, and they may never take the time to watch, read, or listen to the author's interviews. Additionally, there are readers who will not need the epitext to understand the author's intention or commentary on social justice issues. Just as the author and/or publisher do not have to provide epitext, readers can always choose to ignore it. Thus, a change in reader response is dependent on the reader actually needing or reading the epitext in addition to the main text.

> Why might readers decide to seek out or ignore authorial epitext?

Utilizing the epitext, though, has numerous implications for research and teaching. It can allow readers to interact with an author, learn more about the author's background, and see reviews and interpretations of text by other readers. Additionally, as culture is an important aspect of Black authorial production (Bishop, 2007), the epitext can provide essential commentary that gives insight into the author's purpose and can minimize the silencing of Black women writers within the speculative genre and society at large.

To ensure that all readers have access to the essential commentary provided by Black female authors of YA speculative fiction and beyond, there are a few practices educators can consider:

1. Make engaging with the author's website a priority. Too often, the author's online content is disregarded, but if the focus is shifted so that this content is prioritized, an increased level of critical literacy can occur before, during, and after reading.

2. Include author interviews, podcasts, and social media content in the standard curriculum. It is not necessary to have students read or listen to the entirety of this content, but engaging with how authors position their work is essential to better understanding the underlying meanings that guide their writing.

3. Have students conduct research on issues highlighted in the epitext before reading. Clayton references unattainable beauty standards, and Adeyemi discusses institutional violence against Black people. Each of these topics can be further researched so that students have a better understanding of the real-life commentary present in the speculative texts.

Consistently employing these practices can assist students in critically engaging with speculative YA texts written by Black female authors. Importantly, it can also assist students in attaining more tools they can use to grapple with important content in the epitext, the text, and society at large.

Conclusion

The modern world is heavily populated with new textual forms, and as the world has changed, so too have the ways in which authors assert an influence over reader response. Texts now not only include peritextual features that exist within the bound pages of the book, but they also include numerous epitextual features that exist beyond the book. These changes have the potential to drastically alter the ways in which educators conceptualize reader response, as the additional information provides a new way to interpret the theory as more than just a transaction between reader and text, reader and immediate community, or reader and their cultural background.

Genette (1997) argued that epitextual elements can serve various purposes, including intention, interpretation, advice, and command. He also argued that some elements are addressed to the general public, whereas other elements, such as promotional materials, may be addressed to booksellers or critics. In the case of the young adult texts highlighted in this chapter, the paratextual elements are addressed to readers who are less cognizant of the social justice issues that underlie and inform the work. It is an attempt to ensure that the meaning behind one of the major themes is not lost on the reader. It is an endeavor, taken on by the author, to assist readers in reaching a point of shared meaning, where the reader and author align, at least on one aspect of the text.

Reflecting on Your Learning

Should a work be able to stand on its own, or are readers always using personal experience and knowledge to inform their response to a work? How important is it for readers to understand the author's intent when it is not explained or made clear within the work itself? How can authorial epitext be used in diversity coursework to enhance a work's ability to increase background knowledge and empathy in readers?

References

Adeyemi, T. (2018). *Children of blood and bone*. New York: Henry Holt.

Bishop, R. S. (2007). *Free within ourselves: The development of African American children's literature*. Portsmouth, NH: Heinemann.

Clayton, D. (2018a). *The Belles*. New York: Freeform Books.

Clayton, D. (2018b). *Books*. https://www.dhonielleclayton.com/my-books

Dery, Mark. (1994). Black to the future: Interviews with Samuel R. Delany, Greg Tate, and Tricia Rose. In Mark Dery (ed.), *Flame wars: The discourse of cyberculture* (pp. 179–222). Durham, NC: Duke University Press.

Genette, G. (1997). *Paratexts: Thresholds of interpretation*. New York: Cambridge University Press.

Hopkinson, N., & Nelson, A. (2002). "Making the impossible possible": An interview with Nalo Hopkinson. *Social Text, 20*(2): 97–113.

Iser, W. (1972). *The act of reading: A theory of aesthetic response*. Baltimore, MD: Johns Hopkins University Press.

Jarema, K. (2018, February 6). 'The Belles' by Dhonielle Clayton exposes the dark sides of beauty and ambition. *Bustle*. https://www.bustle.com/p /the-belles-by-dhonielle-clayton-exposes-the-dark-sides-of-beauty -ambition-8087446

Jones, J. (2018, May 15). Tomi Adeyemi wanted 'Children of Blood and Bone' to be so good . . . so Black. *Huffington Post*. https://www.huffingtonpost .com/entry/tomi-adeyemi-children-of-blood-and-bone_us_5af5d71ae 4b032b10bfa735f

Leavenworth, M. L. (2015). The paratext of fan fiction. *Narrative, 23*(1): 40–60.

Murray, P. R. (2012). Scott Pilgrim vs the future of comics publishing. *Studies in Comics, 3*(1): 129–142.

Rosenblatt, L. (1978). *The reader, the text, the poem: The transactional theory of the literary work*. Carbondale: Southern Illinois University Press.

Young, R. (2018, July 31). YA author Tomi Adeyemi wants to show Black people "they can be heroes." *WBUR*. http://www.wbur.org/hereandnow /2018/07/31/children-of-blood-and-bone-tomi-adeyemi

Fostering Diverse Learners' Comprehension and Critical Thinking Through Epitext

Loren Jones, Sharon L. Smith, and Luciana C. de Oliveira

Introduction

The 21st century has ushered in not only a myriad of approaches and techniques for elementary teachers to utilize when working with young students who are learning how to read and write, but also new and broadened conceptualizations of what counts as consuming and producing texts. Whereas traditional approaches to literacy learning have centered around the written text, scholarship in this area has expanded to include the important role that paratext can play in developing students' comprehension and critical thinking skills (Gross et al., 2016; Martinez et al., 2016; Sipe, 2008). The paratext is comprised of both the elements that are found within a text (*peritext*) and those that exist outside of a text, but still refer to it (*epitext*) (Genette, 1997). Research has shown that these elements affect how readers interpret and engage with the text (Gross, 2019), often offering them "a richer and more gratifying reading experience" (Coifman, 2013, p. 21).

Statement of Issue to Be Considered

Classrooms across the United States are becoming increasingly diverse, and with this shift in demographics, teachers have been charged with adapting their literacy practices to meet the needs of all their students. In order to do this, some teachers have broadened their scope to integrate components in addition to their focal texts. These epitextual components may include items that deal with the production, promotion, dissemination, reception, extension, and reference of these texts, as discussed in the introduction to this book (p. ix). For example, within the category of dissemination, the teacher may choose to incorporate author interviews or read-alouds to further engage students with the focal text. Alternatively, within the realm of promotion, the teacher may elect to showcase book trailers, print advertisements, or posters to provide students with a more comprehensive view of the text. No matter the category selected, teachers often have the flexibility to present these different epitextual components for students both to consume and to produce. Nevertheless, there appears to be a dearth of research in this area, especially when it comes to emerging bilinguals (EBs).

> Author interviews might also help promote a text. How might author interviews also serve other epitextual functions?

This chapter seeks to explore this area, first examining how one elementary teacher was able to incorporate epitextual components in her instruction and discussing opportunities for making meaning through additional strategies and activities surrounding epitext. The next section situates this work within the functions of epitext, as listed in the introduction to this book (p. ix) and conceptualizes the function around which this chapter is centered: *extension*. Following this conceptual framework, a brief overview of related research is presented. After providing a theoretical foundation for this work and situating it within current work, the largest section of this chapter focuses on practical methods and strategies for applying this approach in the elementary classroom. Though this chapter presents this approach in an elementary context, the ideas included can be adapted to diverse secondary and tertiary settings. This chapter concludes with a discussion of future directions for practice and research.

How the Work Is Situated in Epitext and the Functions of Epitext

One of the six functions of epitext is *extension*. This element affords readers the opportunity to further their comprehension by analyzing and creating related literary materials that extend the focal text in some manner. In their introduction, Witte, Latham, and Gross (p. ix) identify six types of text that make up the extension element. *Sequels and prequels* are books that come before or after a book from a series and share a common theme, expanding on other work by this author and/or illustrator in the series. Texts classified as *parodies* consist of exaggerated, often humorous imitations of an original work. *Pastiche* also imitates original works, but unlike parody, these publications seek to honor the original work. *Fan fiction* extends and/or creates new storylines through "a unique form of writing in which fans base their stories on the characters and plotlines of existing media and popular culture" (Black, 2009, p. 398). *Transmedia* extends stories by using multiple formats and digital platforms to contribute to the story. Lastly, *remix* includes compositions that consistently manipulate different elements from the original text (Stedman, 2012).

Though this area appears to be understudied, an emerging body of work points to this as a promising practice for engaging diverse learners (e.g., Black, 2009; Davila & Patrick, 2010). This chapter specifically focuses on extension through sequels and/or prequels and fan fiction, drawing on the three questions that the editors provide for consideration in the Introduction when one interacts with the extension element of epitexts:

1. How do these elements help you understand the work better?

2. How do readers of a text interact with the text?

3. How does the creation of extension texts honor or critique the primary work?

Review of the Relevant Literature

Although book series, composed of a range of prequels and/or sequels, are a common staple in elementary classrooms, the research that addresses their use, especially with EBs, remains limited. Davila and Patrick (2010) provide a comprehensive overview of the research related to the types of books children choose or report wanting to read, which highlights book series as an overall preference. In various studies, children described how book series encouraged their reading habits as they became engrossed with the characters or in the storyline, which aligns well with previous work from Farris et al. (2009).

In addition to student engagement, this body of research posits that the "narrow reading" of texts by the same author and about the same characters can lay the groundwork for developing reading skills and strategies that students can later expand upon with a wider range of texts and genres (Davila & Patrick, 2010; McQuillan, 2016). Engaging with book series provides students with background knowledge and builds schemas that facilitate access to the story elements and various linguistic features of sequels, including vocabulary (Farris et al., 2009; Hansen & Collins, 2015; McQuillan, 2016). Although there is minimal research on narrow reading through book series with elementary EBs in the United States (Hansen & Collins, 2015), the instructional practices of building background knowledge and providing opportunities for repeated exposure to vocabulary are evidence-based practices critical for the language and literacy development of EBs (Herrera, Perez, & Escamilla, 2015).

Scholarship on fan fiction, the second aspect of extension on which this chapter focuses, also appears to be understudied at the elementary level and with EBs. Nevertheless, there is a small body of work that points to extending books through this epitextual component as a promising practice for scaffolding EBs' language development, especially in terms of writing (e.g., Black, 2009; Jwa, 2012; Li, 2012; Sauro & Sundmark, 2016). Work in this area appears to focus on how EBs have been able to create literary identities for themselves through their fan fiction. Having the freedom to use all their communicative resources, including both artistic depictions and written word in multiple languages, has positioned these learners as experts, validating their multilingual and multicultural identities while developing their competencies in English. Though this activity is promising as a culturally and linguistically sustaining practice, a serious dearth of research still exists in the field.

Context

To further promote teachers' use of the extension component of epitext, this chapter draws on the authors' experiences in a diverse elementary classroom, working collaboratively with a first-grade teacher, Ms. Cabana (pseudonym), to explore specific strategies that educators can use to foster students' critical thinking and comprehension of texts. The authors are a team composed of a university professor (de Oliveira), an assistant clinical professor (Jones), and a classroom teacher (Smith), who were at the time a doctoral candidate and second-year doctoral student. Together, these three authors comprised a research team that worked closely with Ms. Cabana, meeting weekly to share and develop ideas, create materials for literacy lessons, debrief, and analyze collected data.

Grounded in current research and evidence-based best practices vis-à-vis literacy, EBs, and the emerging body of work on epitextual elements, this chapter is centered around two focal texts, demonstrating how extension elements can be utilized in unique ways to the benefit of diverse learners. The two focal texts, *Dolphins at Daybreak* (Osborne, 1997) and *High Tide in Hawaii* (Osborne, 2003), are both part of a series of more than 50 *Magic Treehouse* books that follow two children, Jack and Annie, as they go on exciting adventures, traveling through time and space in a magic treehouse. According to the Accelerated Reader (AR) program, these texts are designated as a level 3.1 and 3.4 respectively, indicating that they could likely be read by a student whose reading skills are similar to those expected of a third-grader during the first and fourth months of school.

> Can you think of other series that are popular with children and that might also be used to help them understand extension elements?

Approach to Using Extension Elements

This section explores practical methods that teachers can employ during literacy instruction to address the epitextual extension elements of sequels and/or prequels and fan fiction. The first part of this section focuses primarily on student consumption of book series, highlighted through examples related to the two aforementioned focal texts. The second part also draws on examples from these texts, but is centered around extension through student production of fan fiction.

Reading Book Series

The importance of being able to understand and to analyze sequels and prequels, a component of the extension epitext, is underscored within the third-grade Common Core reading literature standard *RL.3.9: Compare and contrast the themes, settings, and plots of stories written by the same author about the same or similar characters (e.g., in books from a series)* (National Governors Association Center for Best Practices [NGA] & Council of Chief State School Officers [CCSSO], 2010). This standard, focused on book series, lays the important foundation for the requirements that apply to later grades related to comparing and contrasting texts in similar or different genres (e.g., grades four through six) and analyzing authors' approaches to intertextuality and the way their personal interpretations and positionality are conveyed throughout the work (e.g., grades seven through 12).

Teachers in early elementary grades can purposefully structure lessons to thoughtfully explore the epitextual elements of sequels and prequels in order to promote students' comprehension, critical-thinking, and higher-order skills and to scaffold their language and literacy development. The following excerpt, taken from an audio-recorded instructional session in a first-grade classroom that is part of the authors' ongoing work with scaffolding diverse students' literacy development, shows how Ms. Cabana explored the epitextual elements to advance EBs' literacy learning. Although comparing and contrasting elements of books across a series is a third-grade standard, Ms. Cabana was able to expose the students to this work and challenge them to work toward this standard as they read the books together in a context of high support. Excerpt 1 illustrates how readers of sequels interacted with the texts and how the sequels helped them understand the work better (questions 1 and 2 for the element of extension epitext as provided in the Introduction to this book).

Excerpt 1

Teacher: A *series* is a group of books that go in order from one to however much and then the main characters stay the same. So there are two main characters and then there will be other characters in the story. Who can tell me about the two main characters in this story?

Marco: Annie and the boy.

Teacher: What is the boy's name?

Students: Jack.

Teacher: Who can tell me something about Annie?

Gabriel: She believes in magic.

Teacher: She believes in magic. Okay. So we know Annie believes in magic. What else do we know about her?

Sara: She's smaller than Jack.

Teacher: Do you mean she is younger?

Sara: Yeah.

Teacher: Okay, so she is fast?

Marco: No, she is active.

Teacher: Okay, good. She's active.

In this excerpt, Ms. Cabana engaged students in a preliminary discussion about the new chapter book they would soon be reading, *Dolphins at Daybreak.* Because so many of the students had previous experience with other books in this series, they were able to work together to build a shared knowledge base about the main characters. This knowledge base, stemming from students' existing background knowledge, provided students with a springboard from which they could create additional meanings as they read the new text. As they started to read the new book in the series, the teacher continued to challenge the students to compare and contrast the sequels (see Excerpt 2).

Excerpt 2

Javier: I see something that is the same between *Dolphins at Daybreak* and *High Tide in Hawaii,* and they are both on the water.

Teacher: Good. So, when we talk about where a story takes place, what is that called?

Students: Setting.

Teacher: For the first time, we are reading a book with a prologue. Sara is noticing that it doesn't have a number in front of it. So, what could that mean? We are going to take a look and see if we can figure it out. Then we have 10 chapters, what are some of the chapters you see?

Students: [Read out chapter titles]

Teacher: Okay, in which chapter do you think they land in Hawaii?

Students: "Aloha."

Teacher: Which chapter do you think might have a problem?

Students: "Ride for your Life."

Teacher: What does that remind you of?

Students: "Swim for your Life!" [chapter from *Dolphins at Daybreak*]

Excerpt 2 showcases how students were able to make text-to-text connections between the two focal texts. By using the book cover as a starting point, students were able to find similarities between the settings of the two stories. In addition, they were able to identify

> Book covers are examples of a promotional peritext. For more information about different types of peritext, see Witte, Latham, & Gross (2019), *Literacy Engagement Through Peritextual Analysis* (ALA/NCTE 2019).

common language between two of the key chapters in the books—"Ride for your Life" and "Swim for your Life." Research has shown how critical it is for EBs to have background knowledge prior to engaging with new texts, and text-to-text connections are one way of helping students gain and realize this knowledge (e.g., Herrera et al., 2015).

These excerpts flowed naturally within this elementary classroom; however, teachers can plan reading lessons around the affordances that sequels offer, focusing on how book series help readers become experts on different story elements (e.g., characters, author's craft). Mini-lessons centered around collecting information on characters, thinking about their actions and words, paying attention to how they respond to problems, and noticing what their relationships demonstrate can provide readers with a deep understanding of character traits and character development (Hartman & Calkins, 2015). Teachers may elect to incorporate multimodal supports such as Venn diagrams, anchor charts, and role-playing activities to help students make these connections with the characters across book series. Furthermore, providing mini-lessons that focus on the author's craft (e.g., visualization, word choice, punctuation, layout) can help students not only with reading comprehension, but also with writing strategies (Hartman & Calkins, 2015).

Writing Fan Fiction

When examining book series in the classroom, teachers can plan to incorporate opportunities for extension activities that fall under the broad category of fan fiction. Fan fiction might include extending story lines, creating new narrative threads, developing new relationships between characters, or focusing on underdeveloped characters (Black, 2009). Within the instructional unit focused on *Dolphins at Daybreak*, Ms. Cabana challenged students to position themselves as one of the main characters (Jack) from the series. Specifically, she asked students to write about how they might have handled one of the main problems differently. This writing prompt encouraged students to make text-to-self connections, which can facilitate reading comprehension for EBs (Herrera et al., 2015; see Excerpt 3).

Excerpt 3

Teacher: I'm going to write for you some questions that I want you to think about. When you go answer these questions it's going to make like a paragraph. So, the first thing I want you to tell me is what is Jack and Annie's problem in this chapter, what do they do to solve the problem, how is the problem solved, and if you were Jack, would you have been able to swim calmly?

In addition to this writing activity, the teacher could have further extended students' understanding through the use of text-to-text connections by asking students to apply what they had learned about the characters, setting, and storyline to write an additional chapter or section grounded in their understandings of these elements that had developed throughout the series. After working with these sequels, the teacher could also prompt students to create their own adventure for Jack and Annie that follows the structure of the two stories that were previously read and analyzed in depth. After creating their fan-fiction pieces, the teacher could then work with students to discuss how their writing aligns with that of the series and how their work may be unique and different from what has already been produced. This would provide an opportunity for the teacher to address the third question posed in the Introduction for the element of extension epitext: *How does the creation of extension texts honor or critique the primary work?*

> Students might also work in small groups to create fan fiction, with each student contributing to parts of a larger story. As a variation, some students might contribute writing while others contribute drawings.

Such activities demand higher-order thinking, as students are required to compare and contrast elements across texts, synthesize what they learn about the characters and story structure, and then create a new text that applies and integrates that knowledge. Furthermore, they provide an opportunity to address Common Core writing standards, such as the third-grade standard *W.3.3: Write narratives to develop real or imagined experiences or events using effective technique, descriptive details, and clear event sequences* (NGO & CCSSO, 2010), because fan fiction encompasses narratives with imagined experiences and events, and studying the author's craft provides students with models of effective techniques, descriptive details, and clearly sequenced events.

Implications and Conclusions

This chapter briefly highlighted the current state of research as it relates to a couple of components of extension epitext: sequels and/or prequels and fan fiction. It also presented readers with some practical applications of how these components can be addressed in a reading/English language arts context in an elementary classroom, drawing attention to some instances in which they can specifically support EBs' language and literacy development. While the approach presented provides some practical applications that teachers can use in their instructional practices, it also underscores the need for further research in this area. Future research directions should address both the consumption and the production of the extension elements of epitexts; there is especially a need for scholarship focused on EBs at the elementary level. This chapter demonstrates how utilizing sequels in a series can provide students with high-challenge, yet high-support learning environments. Drawing on students' background knowledge, fostering text-to-self and text-to-text connections, and providing opportunities for meaningful writing activities provide students with critical access to language and English language arts content.

Reflecting on Your Learning

Sequels and prequels and fan fiction are examples of extension elements. What are the key differences between sequels and prequels on the one hand and fan fiction on the other? What is the appeal of series books for children? What is the appeal of fan fiction? Can you think of an activity you might use with children to help them develop promotional epitext for the fan fiction they have written?

References

Black, R. W. (2009). Online fan fiction, global identities, and imagination. *Research in the Teaching of English*, *43*(4): 397–425.

Coifman, R. C. (2013). Giving texts meaning through paratexts: Reading and interpreting endpapers. *School Library Monthly*, *30*(3): 21–23.

National Governor's Association Center for Best Practices, Council of Chief State School Officers. (2010). *Common core state standards (English language arts)*. Washington, DC: National Governor's Association Center for Best Practices, Council of Chief State School Officers. Retrieved from http://www.corestandards.org/ELA-Literacy

Davila, D., & Patrick, L. (2010). Asking the experts: What children have to say about their reading preferences. *Language Arts*, *87*(3): 199. https://library.ncte.org/journals/la/issues/v87-3

Farris, P. J., Werderich, D. E., Nelson, P. A., & Fuhler, C. J. (2009). Male call: Fifth-grade boys' reading preferences. *The Reading Teacher*, *63*(3): 180–188. https://www.jstor.org/stable/25615807

Genette, G. (1997). *Paratexts: Thresholds of interpretation*. Cambridge, UK: Cambridge University Press.

Gross, M. (2019). Grounding our work theoretically: The peritextual literacy framework. In S. Witte, D. Latham, & M. Gross (eds.), *Literacy engagement through peritextual analysis* (pp. 3–16). Chicago, IL: American Library Association & National Council of Teachers of English.

Gross, M., Latham, D., Underhill, J., & Bak, H. (2016). The Peritext book club: Reading to foster critical thinking about STEAM texts. *School Library Research*, *19*: 1–17.

Hansen, L. E., & Collins, P. (2015). Revisiting the case for narrow reading with English language learners. *The Reading Matrix: An International Online Journal*, *15*(2): 137–155. http://www.readingmatrix.com/files/13 -ro1o846k.pdf

Hartman, A., & Calkins, L. (2015). Series book clubs (Reading units of study— grade 2). Portsmouth, NH: Heinemann.

Herrera, S. G., Perez, D. R., & Escamilla, K. (2015). *Teaching reading to English language learners: Differentiated literacies* (2nd ed.). Boston, MA: Allyn & Bacon/Pearson Education.

Jwa, S. (2012). Modeling L2 writer voice: Discoursal positioning in fanfiction writing. *Computers and Composition*, 29: 323–340. https://doi.org/10 .1016/j.compcom.2012.10.001

Li, G. (2012). Literacy engagement through online and offline communities outside school: English language learner's development as readers and writers. *Theory into Practice*, 51: 312–318. https://doi.org/10.1080 /00405841.2012.726061

Martinez, M., Stier, C., & Falcon, L. (2016). Judging a book by its cover: An investigation of peritextual features in Caldecott award books. *Children's Literature in Education*, *47*(3): 225–241.

McQuillan, J. (2016). What can readers read after graded readers? *Reading in a Foreign Language*, *28*(1): 63–78. http://nflrc.hawaii.edu/rfl

Osborne, M. P. (1997). *Magic tree house: Dolphins at daybreak*. New York: Random House Children's Books.

Osborne, M. P. (2003). *Magic tree house: High tide in Hawaii*. New York: Random House Children's Books.

Sauro, S., & Sundmark, B. (2016). Report from middle-earth: Fan fiction tasks in the EFL classroom. *ELT Journal*, *70*(4): 414–423. https://doi.org/10 .1093/elt/ccv075

Sipe, L. R. (2008). *Storytime: Young children's literary understanding in the classroom*. New York: Teachers College Press.

Stedman, K. D. (2012). Remix literacy and fan compositions. *Computers and Composition*, *29*(2): 107–123. https://doi.org/10.1016/j.compcom.2012 .02.002

Witte, S., Latham, D., & Gross, M. (eds.) (2019). *Literacy engagement through peritextual analysis*. Chicago, IL: American Library Association & National Council of Teachers of English.

PART III

Epitext and Media

CHAPTER 8

Creating Epitext and Intertext Perspectives with *Mary Poppins Returns*

Margaret Mackey

Jonathan Gray draws our attention to the ubiquity of the paratext in our current cultural industries, paying particular attention to film and television:

> Paratexts surround texts, audiences, and industry, as organic and naturally occurring a part of our mediated environment as are movies and television themselves. If we imagine the triumvirate of Text, Audience, and Industry as the Big Three of media practice, then paratexts fill the space between them, conditioning passages and trajectories that criss-cross the mediascape, and variously negotiating or determining interactions among the three. (2010, p. 23)

Gray's work is fascinating and informative, but he does not distinguish between *paratexts* (textual devices that frame, present, and/or comment on the main text from within the material and conceptual frame of that work) and the external devices that Genette, mainly discussing books, calls *epitexts*:

> The epitext is any paratextual element not materially appended to the text within the same volume but circulating, as it were, freely, in a virtually

limitless physical and social space. The location of the epitext is therefore anywhere outside the book. (1997/1987, p. 344)

Statement of the Issue to Be Considered

In his very detailed analysis of paratextual and epitextual hierarchies, Genette is dismissive of marketing materials: "I will not dwell on the publisher's epitext: its basically marketing and 'promotional' function does not always involve the responsibility of the author in a very meaningful way; most often he [sic] is satisfied just to close his eyes officially to the value-inflating hyperbole inseparable from the needs of trade" (1987/1997, p. 347). Genette's examples include "[p]osters, advertisements, press releases and other prospectuses . . . , periodical bulletins addressed to book-sellers and 'promotional dossiers' for the use of sales reps. Our media-oriented era will no doubt see other props exploited" (1987/1997, p. 347).

It has been more than 30 years since Genette's study of paratexts was published in France. Both the date and the European context may help to explain the sober nature of his list of publishers' epitexts; most of his examples suggest a context of aids to assist booksellers and librarians with handselling a particular title. Because the author is minimally involved in these commercial extensions of a text, Genette turns loftily away.

For contemporary readers and viewers, especially in the anglophone world, the commercial epitext is not so easily dismissed. From a very early age, readers and viewers learn to locate themselves in relation to a primary text within the context of a riot of secondary epitexts. Gray, in contrast to Genette, is intrigued by the commercial epitext: "Much of the business of media, in both economic and hermeneutic terms, then, is conducted before watching, when hopes, expectations, worries, concerns, and desires coalesce to offer us images and scripts of what the text might be" (2010, pp. 24–25). It is telling that his analysis includes the hermeneutic effect of an apparatus that is often perceived solely in marketing terms.

Context

More than 20 years ago, I made a substantial collection of more than 60 texts all related to the 1997 release of the blockbuster movie *Men in Black* (Mackey 1999, 2001). These already large numbers were hugely augmented by a range of related television programs and Internet sites. Although I was not uninterested in the economic implications of my collection, I mainly focused on the hermeneutic impact of so many renditions, versions, reworkings, and commentaries. To help sort through the kinds of invitation these materials offer to viewers/readers, I developed a schematic outline of seven categories: immersion, recapitulation, second-level engagement, technical analysis, commentary, spin-off, and parody.

My question as I gathered my 1997 materials was the same question I bring to the issue today: What is the impact of such ubiquity of spin-offs, retellings, commodities, collectibles, and associated consumerism on how young people learn to respond to a text? To discuss this question here, I draw on Gray's extensive consideration of commercial materials, but I also make use of Genette's helpful distinction between peritext and epitext. For my case study, I turn to a primary text that came into the world in a context not only of epitextual and peritextual plenty but also of intellectual complexity. My sample text is *Mary Poppins Returns*, a 2018 Disney movie starring Emily Blunt and Lin-Manuel Miranda. This film reflects, riffs on, and speaks back to an earlier Disney movie, *Mary Poppins* (1964), which, in its turn, derives from P. L. Travers's sequence of novels about Mary Poppins, the stern but magical nanny who flies in to help the Banks family when times are hard. In addition to the two movies and the series of books, recent reworkings include a stage musical and a movie about the making of the 1964 film (*Saving Mr. Banks*).

Although the film version of *Men in Black* was adapted from a comic book story, the movie represented the first large-scale telling. In contrast, *Mary Poppins Returns* appears *in medias res* as it were, as part of a complicated ongoing chronicle of adaptation and re-adaptation. As a consequence, the epitexts that feature in this chapter call for an eighth category of readerly invitation: that of bringing readers and viewers up to speed with a complex textual history, of supplying an intertextual repertoire adequate to the occasion of a new installment in the ongoing sequence of telling the story of Mary Poppins.

> Compare the use of nonauthorial epitext to reveal the history of adaptations to a work to Toliver's example of authorial epitext meant to provide cultural insight and to clarify the author's intentions.

In this chapter, I particularly address the discourses of a set of supermarket epitexts that appeared in the lead-up to the release of the film in late 2018. Three of them are dedicated magazines: the *Disney*, Mary Poppins Returns: *Official Collector's Edition* (2018); a *Life* guide to *Mary Poppins: The Magic, the Adventure, the Love* (2018); and *People*'s *The Practically Perfect Guide to Mary Poppins (Commemorative Edition)* (2018). Another major anticipatory publication is *Vogue* magazine's issue of December 2018, which features Emily Blunt in a Poppins-esque costume on the cover and also includes fashion shots of Blunt and co-star Lin-Manuel Miranda and a report on interviews with both of them. Not every epitext is shaped or influenced by Disney's publicity department, of course. I also refer to reviews of the movie on its release, and comment on a more significant critique from the *New York Times* from early in 2019.

Application of Approach

I have written before about the textual universe of the *Mary Poppins* works (Mackey 2016), exploring the complexity of the relationship between the different iterations of the story and its characters. The novels are strikingly open-ended (Mary Poppins comes and goes without making any essential changes to the Banks family), but the 1964 movie imposes a happy ending, particularly in redefining the character of Mr. Banks. In 2016, acknowledging the canonical status of the film and observing how its ending transforms Mr. and Mrs. Banks into loving and attentive parents, I wrote, "If the movie Mary Poppins 'came back' to a logically designed sequel, she would surely discover that there was little left for her to do" (p. 20). The makers of *Mary Poppins Returns* acknowledged this narrative problem and cleverly solved it by jumping ahead a generation. Jane and Michael are now adults, and Michael is the recently widowed father of three children, struggling to build a new life for them in the face of overwhelming grief. Here is a new family in need of Mary Poppins's magic.

> Adaptations can also be identified as extension epitext. Consider the relationship between intertextuality and epitext in describing the reception of texts.

Mary Poppins Returns is a relatively linear story, with a starting point of a family in emotional and financial turmoil and an endpoint of security re-established under both headings. But despite its surface simplicity, this story involves not only paratexts and epitexts, but also intertexts. The layers of Travers's versions and Disney's versions speak to each other; as Hutcheon reminds us, seen from the perspective of the *process of reception*, adaptation is a form of intertextuality: we experience adaptations (as *adaptations*) as palimpsests through our memory of other works that resonate through repetition with variation (2006, p. 8).

Some viewers will bring awareness of the earlier materials to their audience role. To offer the simplest kind of example, the names of the three children in *Mary Poppins Returns* make intertextual reference, not to the 1964 movie in which Jane and Michael were the only Banks children, but to the books, where John was one of twin babies at the start of the saga and baby Annabel joined the family in a later book. Georgie is named for his grandfather, a character in both books and film. Book readers do not really gain any insight into the characters of movie twins John and Annabel by registering this family nomenclature, but there is a small frisson of pleasure at being what Hutcheon calls a "knowing" audience, equipped to participate in a "democratizing kind of straightforward awareness of the adaptation's enriching, palimpsestic doubleness" (2006, p. 120).

As is demonstrated by my simple example of the children's names, however, *Mary Poppins* provides more layers than a "straightforward . . . doubleness," as the 1964 movie made some significant narrative changes to the book material, meaning that contradictions must be folded into any relatively complete palimpsest. Furthermore, knowing viewers of *Mary Poppins Returns* may be aware that these narrative changes are actually the subject matter of another movie, *Saving Mr. Banks*, a film about Travers's resistance to Disney's alterations. As I have discussed elsewhere (Mackey 2016), that movie ends with Travers succumbing to the paternalistic logic of Walt Disney's pop psychology—but as the credits roll, the audiotapes of Travers's own voice providing an acerbic commentary on the alterations to her story remind us that a non-Disney perspective still exists. Outside the world of the film narrative, it also remains possible to trace Travers's negative post-movie reflections through a variety of print sources.

The straightforward narrative arc of the 2018 movie's main plotline permits digressions into the various adventures to which Mary Poppins invites the children. The story of the healing of a bereft family through Mary Poppins's magic is also rendered more elaborate through the assorted intertextual references. Jane and Michael, now grown up, provide the largest-scale intertextual link, but many are smaller and subtler. Musical phrases from the earlier movie are woven into the soundtrack of the new film, for example. Costume designer Sandy Powell describes an artefactual link, a decorative robin on the side of Mary Poppins's hat in the 2018 film:

> I thought of the robin from the original "Spoonful of Sugar" number and I thought that would be funny, to have a robin on the side of her hat. So I went through a process of making lots of different versions of robins and ended up with a beautiful one. It's actually carved from cork and then covered in fabric and completely embroidered and the whole thing is made from thread. (*Disney*, p. 64)

Magical adventures in the sequel run parallel to escapades of the first, and the chimney sweeps of the first movie are mirrored by the leeries (lamplighters) of the new one. Perhaps the most startling reference to the first movie comes embodied in the person of Dick Van Dyke, who reprises his role (also doubled in the 1964 movie with that of Bert the chimney sweep) of old Mr. Dawes—though on this occasion, in keeping with the passage of time since the first film, he is Dawes Jr. rather than Dawes Sr., his original character.

There are many examples of such parallels; it is arguable that the songs are also doubled. Clark observes,

> Like the original film's music, every single song on the Mary Poppins Returns soundtrack is an immediate earworm. But even more than that, nearly every song in the sequel is an analogue to a song in the original, and pushes the plot forward precisely in the same way. If you're curious, it's worth examining the two soundtracks side by side to compare titles and concepts. (2018, para. 3)

The main story is simple and sentimental, and the side excursions are light-hearted and colorful. Immersion in the family's sadness and recovery is one completely appropriate response. Yet viewers with an appropriate repertoire of other Poppins texts may bring a more complex interpretive stance to the story. Even a little bit of background knowledge about the books, the 1964 film, the stage musical, and the meta-story of *Saving Mr. Banks* will establish a very clear sense that this story is a construction and that some elements are simply incompatible. Such complexity permits the Disney corporation to have its cake and eat it too: at one level, we may experience a simple story with hummable tunes; at another level not very far away, and carefully signposted by assorted epitexts, a complex and contradictory set of narratives offers the kinds of narrative self-questioning we have come to expect in contemporary culture.

The Magazine Epitexts of *Mary Poppins Returns*

Contemporary children are familiar with such complexity from their early texts, as Serafini and Reid's account of transgressive boundary-breaking in picture books makes very clear (2019). They say,

> Exposing the constructed nature of fiction and showing how texts work reveals the innately human act of storytelling. Behind every text exist real-world authors, illustrators, and publishers who design narratives according to particular conventions of representation, communication, and dissemination practices. Single, stable, universal truths are not presented in these narratives, just as they do not exist in the culture in which young readers are embedded. (2019, Discussion section, para. 3)

The epitexts for *Mary Poppins Returns* that I am examining here do an excellent job of presenting information to support Serafini and Reid's assertions, but they stand separate from the narrative world of the film, which has been so carefully crafted and singularly organized.

In the case of the movie of *Mary Poppins Returns*, the intertextual layers may serve to open up contradictory readings of this simple story. The supermarket special issue magazines offer intertextual support in epitextual form. As well as providing tantalizing glimpses of scenes from the upcoming film (easy to keep and return to as a souvenir after the movie opens), all three of them supply a kind of digest version of intertextual repertoire. This particular set of promotional epitexts frames the new movie as something best interpreted in the context of references to prior renditions of the character and world of Mary Poppins. Each of them supplies a repertoire sufficient to create what might be called a *knowing-enough* viewer; additionally, the magazines all recognize that playing among the intertexts is pleasing in its own right for many readers.

The *Vogue* article works from a slightly different perspective, with its nine pages of lush fashion photographs of Blunt and Miranda and the accompanying article, just one-third as long, at three pages. But even this brief account dwells on the play of intertextualities:

> Miranda began his Poppins prep by watching the '64 movie for the first time since his boyhood. . . . Blunt took a different tack. Banishing her self-doubt, she made the executive decision *not* to rewatch the '64 film, which she, too, had last seen in childhood. (Kamp, 2018, p. 127)

Instead, Blunt "immerse[d] herself" (p. 127) in the Travers books. Kamp discusses the artistic consequences of this choice:

> In the books, the title character is severe and forbidding, with some anti-heroic traits such as overweening vanity. . . . and a steadfast refusal to discuss her inner life.

> No surprise then, that the Mary Poppins that emerged from Blunt's preparations is more tart, clipped, and expressly comic than Andrews's. (Kamp, 2018, p. 127)

Explicit references to the earlier versions of the story thus combine with the kind of implicit intertextuality embodied in how the actors prepared themselves for the new film. Such complexity is subsumed in recognizable forms of marketing discourse.

The supermarket magazines with access to lavish stills from the upcoming movie are largely invested in whetting viewers' appetites with relatively uncritical commentary. The three magazines provide slightly different points of focus. The *Life* issue concentrates mainly on the 1964 film, with only a few pages toward the end devoted to the sequel (*Mary Poppins,* 2018). Much of the magazine is dedicated to outlining the differing perspectives of Walt Disney and Pamela Travers (the disagreements that constitute the plot of *Saving Mr. Banks,* though this movie does not feature in the discussion). The *People* version focuses much more intently on the new film, with more than 60 pages of background information, interviews with actors, commentary on special effects, and the like (*Practically perfect,* 2018). Twenty pages offer background on the first movie, and a few pages at the end introduce P. L. Travers and point to other incarnations of *Mary Poppins* over the years. The Disney *Official Collector's Edition* (2018) focuses largely on the new film, but does offer two pages on the books and two pages on how people working in the new movie remember the original film.

> Does promotional epitext support believing versus critical thinking as a stance toward a work? Is believing versus critical thinking a characteristic of the reader or the epitext?

Not surprisingly, there is an overlap of content as well as of themes and topics. For example, here is Angela Lansbury (the Balloon Lady) on what is different about working in a Disney movie: "You have to believe. You have to believe in the magic. You have to believe in all of the qualities that I think most of the Disney movies are infused with. It's all imagination. They never make a dull movie. They don't know how" (*Practically perfect,* p. 43). An almost identical quote appears on page 57 of the official Disney magazine. Both renditions strongly reinforce the popular idea that the appropriate response to a Disney movie is to eliminate your critical thinking apparatus and simply revel in the "magic." "Believing" is the approved stance, rather than, say, "thinking" or "critiquing."

Such epitexts, in Gray's terms, "condition our entrance to texts, telling us what to expect, and setting the terms of our 'faith' in subsequent transubstantiation" (2010, p. 25). In telling us what to expect, such epitexts "shape the reading strategies that we will take with us 'into' the text, and they provide the all-important early frames through which we will examine, react to, and evaluate textual consumption" (2010, p. 26). Gray confirms Meek's seminal observation that "texts teach what readers learn" (1988), but his category of what constitutes a text relevant to the reading experience is more capacious. These magazines offer accounts of Mary Poppins's antecedents that are plural but not critical. Their descriptions of how artistic decisions were achieved are exceedingly respectful and/or admiring.

The Review Epitexts of *Mary Poppins Returns*

The reviews that followed the release of the movie are considerably more diverse in the range of opinions offered. Some critics believe that the nostalgia-heavy emphasis of the 2018 film is successful: "a cinematic delight . . . visual dessert" (Clark, 2018, para. 4); Emily Blunt is "practically perfect in every way" (Noveck, 2018, para. 2). In the normally skeptical *Observer* of London, Mark Kermode buys into the "magic" thesis in a big way. The 1964 film, he says, "touched me deeply as a child and affected me even more profoundly as a father. Just listening to the soundtrack still reduces me to floods of joyful tears" (2018, para. 1). He is thrilled to discover that, despite his trepidation that the new film would not live up to the old, he is captivated by Blunt singing "The Place Where Lost Things Go," "a heartbreaking lullaby that has something of the spine-tingling melancholy charm of Feed the Birds. Watching this sequence, I noticed I had started crying, and realized that I was safe—the movie's spell was working and the magic was still here" (2018, para. 9).

> Reviews often serve the reception function of epitext. Try comparing promotional epitext to reception epitext for similarities and differences.

Not every critic was so impressed. Consider this example from the *Washington Post*:

> "Mary Poppins Returns" works hard to evoke the undeniable charms of the original 1964 film. It replicates many of them in slavish fashion. . . .
>
> I mean, homage is one thing, but this reeks less of nostalgia than sweat. There is so little tolerance for spontaneity, in a film that feels calibrated to the millimeter to be magical, that reactions like delight and surprise—when they occur at all—feel manufactured. (O'Sullivan, 2018, paras. 1–2)

The Guardian of London was equally unconvinced:

> With pastel/primary colours of headspinning prettiness and all-new showtunes polished to a gleam, this sequel to the 1964 Disney standard Mary Poppins is an almost scarily accomplished clone-pastiche of the original, a spoonful of state-of-the-art genetically modified sweetener. (Bradshaw, 2018, para. 1)

Reviews, of course, by their very nature, express personal opinions, and it is not surprising that one person's "charming" is another person's "saccharine." While they open the door to more plurality than the marketing epitexts ever countenance, they each express a singular point of view. A more substantiated confrontation with the whole Mary Poppins enterprise came in the *New York Times* in January 2019, and it is perhaps fitting that the scope of the attack was thoroughly intertextual in nature.

The Sociocultural Epitexts of *Mary Poppins Returns*

Daniel Pollack-Pelzner raises the troubling history of blackface "throughout the Mary Poppins canon, from P. L. Travers's books to Disney's 1964 adaptation, with disturbing echoes in the studio's newest take on the material" (2019, para. 2). He begins by describing the new film as "enjoyably derivative" (para. 1) before recalling that "[o]ne of the more indelible images from the 1964 film is of Mary Poppins blacking up" (para. 3). When she gets covered in chimney soot, she powders her face even blacker before singing and dancing across the London rooftops. "This," says Pollack-Pelzner, "might seem like an innocuous comic scene if Travers's novels didn't associate chimney sweeps' blackened faces with racial caricature" (para. 4), and he goes on to cite references in the novels to support this assertion.

Pollack-Pelzner teases out a thread of racist discourse as complex and intricate as any of the book/movie intertexts discussed so vigorously elsewhere.

> In Travers's first "Mary Poppins" novel, published in 1934, a magic compass transports the children around the world, including a stop where they meet a scantily clad "negro lady," dandling "a tiny black pickaninny with nothing on at all." . . . She addresses Mary Poppins in minstrel dialect and invokes the convention of blacking up: "My, but dem's very white babies. You wan' use a li'l bit black boot polish on dem." (2019, para. 7)

The chapter featuring this adventure was controversial even at the time and Travers eventually rewrote it. "In Travers's 1981 revision, the "negro lady" became a hyacinth macaw who speaks genteel English" (Pollack-Pelzner, 2019, para. 9). This bird makes a cameo appearance in the 2018 film, when Mary Poppins sings a music hall song, "A Cover Is Not the Book." One verse mentions a wealthy widow named Hyacinth Macaw, who is naked: "Blunt sings that 'she only wore a smile,' and Miranda chimes in, 'plus two feathers and a leaf'" (2019, para. 10).

Making intertextual connections in ways validated by much of the pre-release marketing discourses and drawing on visual as well as verbal references, Pollack-Pelzner points out,

> In the 1981 revision of "Mary Poppins," there's no mention of her attire; you'd have to go back to the 1934 original to find the "negro lady" with "a

very few clothes on," sitting under a palm tree with a "crown of feathers." There's even a straw hut behind Blunt and Miranda that replicates Mary Shepard's 1934 illustration. (The hut was removed in the 1981 revision.) (2019, para. 11)

He recounts the role of blackface minstrelsy in the Travers books and also in assorted Disney musicals, troubling the image of the "magic" machine in a compelling act of intertextual connection. This epitext, rather than advertising or supporting or presenting an individual opinion, challenges the foundations of the whole enterprise of retelling. The palimpsest is an ugly one.

Epitexts "shape [our] reading strategies," says Gray, and "provide the all-important early frames through which we will examine, react to, and evaluate textual consumption" (2010, p. 26). This *New York Times* critique will, for many people, come after they have seen the movie on its first release, and it is possible that its "shaping" of our responses may be retroactive. But its intertextual tracking of references is all the more convincing in light of how viewers have been "trained" by the marketing discourses to consider the Poppins universe as multiple and indeterminate, drawing interpretive possibilities out of the complexity of the options regarding the origin tale.

Theory to Practice

Mary Poppins Returns and a few related texts provide a case study of how a singular text may be buttressed by assorted epitexts—and also how an epitext may challenge the character of that text, undermining its claim to be simple and wholesome family entertainment. It is worth remembering that the entire Mary Poppins canon constitutes material considered to be—and marketed as—children's texts. A classroom discussion of the role and significance of epitexts would draw on a roomful of experienced young epitext consumers; the scope for articulating and sometimes challenging many tacit assumptions is very clear.

There are many ways to organize such a discussion. Children as young as the middle elementary years could check out Google and Amazon sites to tally the range of associated texts and consumables for a current or upcoming film. A classroom document camera means that a group could consider how different epitexts frame the viewing experience, at the modest expense of acquiring a single copy of a magazine or two. With a computer and a projector, online previews and reviews both offer resources for analysis, and so do fan art and fan film versions. Students could create their own fan trailers and then explain how they intend to guide viewer response through their framing decisions. Such conversations could happen in real time, as the film is released, or the documentation could be stored until the movie appears in a form usable in the classroom, either in whole or in extract form. Classroom conversations on this theme would articulate a very rich store of implicit knowledge—not necessarily so much about the particular film in question, but rather about the nature of epitext more broadly.

A close consideration of the promotional work of framing response in assorted epitexts can be scaled to the age and abilities of the students involved. My own graduate classes of pre-service librarians could benefit from this kind of work, and so could older elementary students, as well as everybody in between. Raw material is plentiful and it takes very little effort to make lessons very current. Students of every age bring broad background knowledge to the task. Almost any consideration of epitext opens the door to an expanding form of critical discussion.

In short, the exploration of epitexts draws on a ubiquitous element of contemporary culture, makes use of plentiful and cheap or free examples, and may readily lead to more complex consideration of the constructed nature of a text. As the example of *Mary Poppins Returns* shows us, paying attention to the framing work of the epitexts may lead us deep into the heart of critical response.

Reflecting on Your Learning

Have you had the experience of feeling like a "knowing" audience member when engaging with a work? What kind of epitext contributed to your feeling "in the know"? What are the potential pitfalls when epitext extends, adapts, or alters an original work?

References

Bradshaw, P. (2018, December 12). A spoonful of state-of-the-art genetically modified sweetener. [Review of the film *Mary Poppins returns* produced by Disney]. *The Guardian*. https://www.theguardian.com/film/2018/dec/12/mary-poppins-returns-review-sequel-emily-blunt

Clark, N. (2018, December 12). *Mary Poppins returns* is the ultimate nostalgia film for burnt-out millennials. [Review of the film *Mary Poppins returns* produced by Disney]. *Vice*. https://www.vice.com/en_us/article/ev3knw/mary-poppins-returns-is-the-ultimate-nostalgia-film-for-burnt-out-millennials

Disney Mary Poppins Returns: Official collector's edition. (2018). New York: Topix Media Lab.

Genette, G. (1987/1997). *Paratexts: Thresholds of interpretation* (J. E. Lewin, trans). Cambridge, UK: Cambridge University Press.

Gray, J. (2010). *Show sold separately: Promos, spoilers, and other media paratexts.* New York: New York University Press.

Hutcheon, L. (2006). *A theory of adaptation.* New York: Routledge.

Kamp, D. (2018, December). Popp style. [Photographs by Annie Leibovitz]. *Vogue,* 123–135.

Kermode, M. (2018, December 23). Not totally expialidocious but still a joy. [Review of the film *Mary Poppins returns* produced by Disney]. *The Observer.* https://www.theguardian.com/film/2018/dec/23/mary -poppins-returns-review-emily-blunt-rob-marshall-ben-whishaw-lin -manuel-miranda

Mackey, M. (1999). Popular culture and sophisticated reading: *Men in black. English in Education, 33*(1): 47–57.

Mackey, M. (2001, February). Literacy in the zone of corporate development: The cultural and commercial world of *Men in black. Simile: Studies in Media and Information Literacy Education 1*(1). https://www .researchgate.net/publication/251011637_Literacy_in_the_Zone_of _Corporate_Development_The_Cultural_and_Commercial_World _of_Men_in_Black#fullTextFileContent

Mackey, M. (2016). Rules and rhizomes: A Mary Poppins sampler. *Papers: Explorations into Children's Literature, 24*(1): 1–29.

Mary Poppins: The magic, the adventure, the love. (2018). New York: Time Inc.

Meek, M. (1988). *How texts teach what readers learn.* Stroud, UK: Thimble Press.

Noveck, J. (2018, December 12). Spit spot! Blunt's a practically perfect Poppins. [Review of the film *Mary Poppins returns* produced by Disney]. Associated Press. https://www.apnews.com/067adb4e487b4a1fb6305 ba08a3679ffb

O'Sullivan, M. (2018, December 14). "Mary Poppins Returns" desperately wants to be liked, and the result is pretty much joyless. [Review of the film *Mary Poppins returns* produced by Disney]. *Washington Post.* https:// www.washingtonpost.com/goingoutguide/movies/mary-poppins -returns-desperately-wants-to-be-liked-and-the-result-is-pretty-much -joyless/2018/12/14/4fecc832-fe5d-11e8-ad40-cdfd0e0dd65a_story .html?arc404=true

Pollack-Pelzner, D. (2019, January 28). Mary Poppins, and a nanny's shameful flirting with blackface. *New York Times.* https://www.nytimes.com /2019/01/28/movies/mary-poppins-returns-blackface.html

The practically perfect guide to Mary Poppins (Commemorative ed.). (2018). *People.*

Serafini, F., & Reid, S. F. (2019, March 2). Crossing boundaries: Exploring metaleptic transgressions in contemporary picturebooks. *Children's Literature in Education,* First Online. https://doi.org/10.1007/s10583 -019-09382-9

Applying Media Literacy to Promotional Epitexts

Are They Selling Molasses, Falafels, or Books?

Shanedra D. Nowell

Today is the day! The middle school book fair towers over the low library shelves, and the students' excitement is palpable. Watching students wander throughout the room, browsing the books, posters, and other paraphernalia, one begins to wonder if they are truly prepared. Not to read the books they choose, but to critically think about the choices they will make as consumers, today and in the future. How can teachers prepare students to become not only literate, but also media-literate? From book fairs, to video book previews, to blockbuster films based on popular young adult novels, media literacy education asks teachers, students, and all media consumers to consider the ways various forms of promotional messages influence consumers.

Described as the "ability to access, analyze, evaluate, create, and act using all forms of communication," media literacy education "empowers

> Consider how promotional epitext may also persuade people to borrow a particular book (from a library, for instance) and/or recommend a book to others.

people to be critical thinkers and makers, effective communicators, and active citizens" by teaching them the skills to effectively deconstruct and create media messages (National Association for Media Literacy Education, n.d., para. 3). As one of the functions of epitext, the promotion of texts prompts educators and students to analyze the choices authors and publishers make to convince them to buy a book, whether in spaces such as book fairs or bookstores, in print advertisements, or online with websites or promotional videos. By connecting epitext and media literacy, students learn to analyze the text itself, as well as the messages and techniques advertisers use to promote the text. Students are also asked to consider effects or results of these messages on them as readers and consumers.

Merging the author's background in advertising and marketing, experience as a classroom teacher, and current role as a teacher education professor and media literacy researcher, this chapter offers curricular examples to demonstrate how elementary, middle, and high school students can apply the principles of media literacy and epitextual analysis to better understand advertisements and other promotional materials as types of public epitext. Using print advertisements and video book trailers as both targets of media analysis and mentor texts, students can learn the anatomy of advertisements, identify the persuasion techniques used to capture their attention, and develop these skills to respond with their own media creations.

Media Literacy Education

As a 21st-century literacy skill, understanding media literacy is essential to living in today's media-saturated society. Teaching media literacy involves critical thinking, questioning, and analyzing the media encountered each day. The National Association for Media Literacy Education (NAMLE) developed six core principles to anchor the study of media literacy:

1. Media Literacy Education requires active inquiry and critical thinking about the messages we receive and create.

2. Media Literacy Education expands the concept of literacy to include all forms of media (i.e., reading and writing).

3. Media Literacy Education builds and reinforces skills for learners of all ages. Like print literacy, those skills necessitate integrated, interactive, and repeated practice.

4. Media Literacy Education develops informed, reflective and engaged participants essential for a democratic society.

5. Media Literacy Education recognizes that media are a part of culture and function as agents of socialization.

6. Media Literacy Education affirms that people use their individual skills, beliefs and experiences to construct their own meanings from media messages. (NAMLE, 2010, para. 3)

These principles drive NAMLE's "Key Questions" for media analysis (2013), which offer teachers and students ways to decode, deconstruct, and question all types of media messages, including advertisements. As the core principles state, critical thinking, inquiry, and engagement are central components of media literacy education, and the Key Questions provide teachers and students with examples of how to enact media literacy practices in the classroom. For example, the question "Who made this message and why?" tackles authorship and the author's purpose, to help students understand that most advertising messages are created by marketing teams that want to influence them or prod them to buy a product. In a world where youth encounter dozens of YouTube commercials, Internet radio jingles, and clothing logos every day, students often struggle to understand that unseen companies pay millions of dollars to vie for every second of their attention.

This chapter focuses on using inquiry questions to jump-start media analysis in the classroom, including "Who is the target audience?" and "What creative techniques are used and how do they communicate the message?" (NAMLE, 2013) (Table 9-1).

These Key Questions pair well with the promotional function of epitext, as they encourage students to question the ways advertisers promote texts. For promotional epitexts such as book trailers or print flyers, students should consider if the ad is "true to the text itself" and how it "affect[s] your view of the work." Utilizing both the NAMLE Key Questions and the functions of epitext, teachers can prepare their students to dig deeper into the messages within promotional texts and analyze the purposes, credibility, meanings, and the effects these materials have on readers. Using media literacy concepts to anchor the study of promotional epitext, the following sections offer teachers examples of how to explore authors and audiences, messages and meaning, representations and reality, as

These questions and others are presented in the introduction to this book.

Table 9-1: Questions for Analyzing Promotional Epitext Through Media Literacy

Media Literacy Concepts	Media Analysis Questions	Promotional Epitext Analysis Questions
Authors and Audience	• Who made this message and why? • Who is the target audience? • What does this message want me to do? • What should I do in response to this message?	• What do they tell you about the intended audience for the text?
Messages and Meanings	• What creative techniques are used and how do they communicate the message? • What is the message and what ideas or values are implied? • How might a different audience/person interpret the message?	• How do these elements affect your view of the work? Are they interesting? Convincing? Effective? • How do they attempt to make the text appealing? • What do these elements tell you about the text's content?
Representations and Reality	• Is the message credible? Is it fact or opinion? • How credible is this (and how do you know)? • What [or who] are the sources of information, ideas, or assertions? • Can I trust this source to tell me the truth about this topic?	• Is the promotion of the text true to the text itself?

Adapted from NAMLE's *Key Questions* (2013), and Latham, Gross, & Witte's functions of epitext as described in the introduction to this book.

well as ideas for student-created advertisements as assessments in their own classroom.

Who Made this Promotional Message and Why? Understanding Authors and Audience

The first step in analyzing promotional texts is understanding that all media messages, including advertisements, are carefully created by an individual or team in order to move an audience to act in some way. As mentioned before, students often struggle with this concept simply because they are not the ones paying for the message. Students may assume that authorship of promotional text is clear-cut because the name of the book's author(s) is printed on the cover, but book authors rarely serve as the authors or creators of the promotional texts, or advertisements, of their books.

Scholastic, the multidimensional media company, could serve as a great example of this concept for elementary and middle school students. They may know Scholastic through school book fairs or the grade-level specific book flyers, but do they realize Scholastic also publishes some of their favorite series, such as *Harry Potter* (Rowling, 1998), *The Hunger Games* (Collins, 2008), and *The 39 Clues* (Riordan, 2008)? Scholastic also owns the video production companies behind *The Magic School Bus* (Jacobs, 1994) and *Clifford The Big Red Dog* (Over, 2000) television series. The company's website boasts that it is "the world's largest publisher and distributor of children's books with $1.6 billion in annual revenue" and more than "8,400 employees serving customers in more than 165 countries" (Scholastic Asia, 2020, para. 1). With all this publishing power, author J. K. Rowling, for example, does not need to put together her own promotional materials, such as the *Harry Potter* series website (https://kids.scholastic.com/kids/books/harry-potter) or series book trailer (https://youtu.be/s8zBR1l4Tgc).

After viewing these promotional texts, students should ask questions about authors and audiences, such as "Who made this website and why?" or "What does the video book trailer want me to do?" To dive into a deeper understanding of audience, it may be worthwhile to show how Scholastic markets books and other materials to different grade levels with their print and digital book flyers. For example, there is a noticeable difference between the appearance and content of the Kindergarten! and the YA Teens book flyers that most students, grades 5 and up, will recognize. Having students analyze and compare the contents of the book flyers by titles, genres, and types of products could help them answer the question "What does this flyer tell you about the intended audience for the books included in it?" For example, students can point out the differences in colors used. Flyers for younger students display more primary colors (red, blue, and yellow), whereas those designed for teens utilize more sophisticated colors and graphic design patterns in Honolulu and Imperial blues, Verdigris, Celadon green, and turquoise. Distinctions are also seen in the ways the books and other products are displayed. The books listed in YA Teens flyers appeal to adolescents and young adults, such as *Hatchet* (1986) by Gary Paulsen, a Newbery Award-winning text that is a staple on middle school reading lists. Scholastic Book flyers often offer books at discount prices, which appeals to middle school parents and teachers. For the younger audience, the Kindergarten! book flyer features various picture books, including some based on Disney's *Frozen*. Although *Frozen* fans come from all age groups, students can easily identify the audience for this book as beginning readers. By developing an understanding of audience and authorship, students can begin to identify ways in which advertisers target different groups using specific messages and techniques.

What Creative Techniques Are Used and How Do They Communicate the Message? Analyzing Messages and Meaning

Once students understand that most promotional messages are made by creative marketing teams to sell books or other texts, they can learn to pinpoint how buyers are persuaded. Print book advertisements and video book trailers provide the best examples for students to learn the anatomy of advertisements. Beginning with print or static Internet ads, students learn to identify and interpret the headline, copy (any words or descriptions in the ad), fine print (the tiny text that may contain claims, benefits, or disclaimers), and the art/graphics. After learning to identify these elements in print or static Internet ads, students can graduate to analyzing video book trailers to see if they can then recognize these same elements. Another helpful classroom activity is to compare how using animation or video enhances (or weakens) how the message is communicated.

Media analysis asks students not only to identify what creative techniques attract their attention (e.g., colors, music, actors, sound effects, art, headline, or taglines used), but also to evaluate and understand how and why these techniques work. One way to achieve this in a classroom is by teaching advertising appeals. Considered part of an advertiser's message strategy (the overall approach of the advertisement), advertising appeals elicit a consumer's need or desire for a product (Wells, Burnett, & Moriarty, 2006, p. 340). Similar to rhetorical appeals, advertising appeals come in two forms: emotional (pathos) and rational (logos/ethos). Emotional appeals in print and video promotional texts target psychological needs for love, friendship, and social status, as well as our insecurities such as fear, rejection, or the need for safety. In contrast, rational advertising appeals speak to our practical reasoning skills, thoughts, and beliefs (Clow & Baack, 2005; Wells et al., 2006). Having students view, discuss, and analyze print ads and video book trailers to identify elements of ads and advertising appeals prepares them to mimic these moves and techniques in their own media creations.

In an elementary classroom, one could practice this type of epitextual analysis with promotional materials related to the best-selling *I Survived* series by Lauren Tarshis (2010–2020) With more than 20 books widely marketed to young readers, this historical fiction series presents lots of opportunities for analysis. A social media ad for the 2019 release *I Survived The Great Molasses Flood, 1919* provides an example of a print advertisement that students can use to identify the headline, copy, and art (Scholastic Canada, 2019).

Students should ask, "What do the ad's elements say about the book and its context?" and "How do they attempt to make the text appealing?" as they analyze the print advertisement and its advertising appeals (NAMLE, 2013). In answering these questions, students should identify "I Survived" as the headline, with its large, bold print that readers of the series would recognize from book covers. Other recognizable elements include the ad's

> These questions and others are presented in the introduction to this book.

copy and art. *Copy* refers to the central body of text included in a print advertisement. In this ad, the copy reads, "The thrilling *New York Times* bestselling series continues! 100 years ago a killer wave of molasses struck a crowded Boston neighborhood. Who can outrun one of history's strangest disasters?" (Scholastic Canada, para. 4).

Sharing the overall message of the ad, the copy attempts to persuade the viewer with a rational appeal by touting the series' awards and positioning the book as historically authoritative. The ad's copy also appeals to the reader's emotional need for adventure and excitement. The art includes a large image of *The Great Molasses Flood* book and smaller cover images from 18 other books in the *I Survived* series. Along with the "new" sticker graphic on the large cover and the "Stock Up Now!" tag-

> Promotional text often makes use of reception elements, such as awards, honors, and excerpts from positive reviews.

line at the bottom, the cover art and text communicate a sense of urgency and excitement to the viewer (Scholastic Canada, 2019). The "30 Million Books in Print" statistic reminds potential readers of the series' success and its popularity, blending a rational appeal with an emotional, bandwagon appeal (Scholastic Canada, 2019, para. 1). The official book trailer offers elementary students another promotional text to explore (https://youtu.be/_Xw49pmXH5A) as it employs a purely emotional appeal. The

> Students can create their own promotional elements, but they can also create parodies of "official" promotional elements, thus creating extension texts.

opening headline uses sparks and flames to portray excitement as the series refresher reel appeals to the reader's nostalgia for the books. The animation, voiceover, and gurgling molasses sound effect offer creative techniques not found in the static print advertisements. Comparing and contrasting the print and video promotional texts, elementary students should be able to discuss "how these elements affect their view of the book." With this knowledge and understanding of advertising elements and appeals, even the youngest students can more effectively play the role of book promoters and create their own book advertisements and video trailers.

Is the Promotional Message Credible? Decoding Representations and Reality

This final media literacy concept urges students to question the credibility, or trustworthiness, of promotional messages. Students learn to distinguish between fact and opinion within texts, but how does a teacher approach this concept when advertising utilizes opinions to promote products? To evaluate the credibility of promotional texts, students should ask these four media analysis questions:

1. Is this fact, opinion, or something else?

2. How credible is this (and how do you know)?

3. What (or who) are the sources of information, ideas, or assertions?

4. Can I trust this source to tell me the truth about this topic? (NAMLE, 2013).

Applying these questions to book trailers, print advertisements or flyers, and other promotional texts, such as websites and video previews, pushes students past their own assumptions to explore who is behind the promotional message.

In a middle or high school classroom, students could research Internet sites promoting their favorite books or authors. RickRiordan.com and ReadRiordan.com are the official websites for the author behind the Percy Jackson series (Riordan, 2005) and other mythology-driven young adult books. Each website serves as a promotional text, with colorful covers, sales awards, and positive reviews of Riordan's titles, but browsing these sites also reveals several other types of promotional texts, such as bookmarks, character cards, book trailers, and video previews. As an investigation of credibility, students should question the exclusive use of positive reviews or opinions to persuade them as readers and consumers. To entice readers to buy Riordan's recent book *The Trials of Apollo: The Tyrant's Tomb* (Riordan, 2019), marketers employ positive reviews of the book as a message strategy.

> Teachers can also encourage students to try to find less-than-positive reviews, compare them to the positive reviews, and explain why they might or might not read a particular book based on having read the reviews.

One ad on a popular Internet bookseller's site includes a positive review for Riordan's book, calling it "a clash of mythic intrigues and centuries of pop culture to thrill die-hard and new fans alike" (Amazon, "From the Publisher" section, n.d.). Here advertisers apply an emotional appeal with this tactic, wanting the consumer to feel the need to jump on the bandwagon with other readers or suffer from FOMO (the fear of missing out) if they do not buy into the promotional message. Applying media literacy, students can identify the persuasive techniques used and decipher whether or not they should trust the reviews posted. Students should question why unfavorable reviews are not included and how this omission could affect their opinions of the text. After asking the media analysis questions discussed earlier, students can compare the opinions offered as reviews with the author's own take on his work in the video preview of *The Trials of Apollo: The Tyrant's Tomb* (https://youtu.be/7T8zkdRnWAw). Does asking who is behind the promotional message (the book author or a book reviewer) change the trustworthiness of the message in their minds?

As students learn to evaluate credibility, epitextual analysis reminds them to question representation in promotional texts as well. Students should ask if the advertisement, book trailer, or other type of promotional text is "true to the text" it claims to promote. Sometimes book trailers fail this test because they do not present much information about "the book and its contents at all," or focus too much on humor, artistry, or simply making a mini-movie and do little to promote the book (Weinberger, 2016, para. 3). Many of the book trailers promoting Rick

> For more on this, see the introduction to this book.

Riordan's books appear to fail this truth test. For example, the humorous 80-second official trailer for *Magnus Chase and the Gods of Asgard: The Ship of the Dead* (Riordan, 2017) has more to do with the main character's favorite food—falafels—than it does with the plot of the book (https://youtu.be/AaRiaDTVERg). An analysis of three 30-second book trailers for *The Trials of Apollo: The Hidden Oracle* (Riordan, 2016) encounter a similar flaw, as they reveal little about the books and focus more on the main character's funny failings as a fallen Greek god turned mortal (https://www.youtube.com/watch?v=6eW3_1qDbi8&list=PLrVg OYFyR97cZa8detWez97TfO1pPABRv&index=13). While students may enjoy watching and creating book trailers, these ads provide examples of promotional texts ripe for media literacy and epitextual analysis. Working with books and book trailers can help students gain a better understanding of the creative techniques used to influence them as readers and consumers.

Applying Media Literacy and Epitextual Analysis to Student-Created Promotional Texts

One of the main goals of media literacy education is to prepare students to respond to media messages through their own media creations. The analysis exercises presented in this chapter prepare students to apply their knowledge of how advertisements are constructed, how advertising appeals work, and how different audiences are targeted to the creation of print book flyers, posters, or video book trailers. Student-created print advertisements provide a way to assess elementary, middle, or high school students on many concepts. Teachers wanting their students to create video book trailers should be prepared to teach script writing, storyboarding, and using editing software or apps in addition to the media literacy skills (Nowell, 2019). Both book flyers/posters and book trailers offer an alternative to the traditional book report (Wickline, 2011). These types of projects assess students' content knowledge, as well as media literacy and epitextual analysis skills.

Conclusion

Marketing experts estimate that the average person living in the United States encounters between 4,000 and 10,000 advertisements each day in the classroom, at home, and in digital spaces (Simpson, 2017). Education in the 21st century must include media literacy skills and teach students to decipher, decode, and create all forms of media. This chapter explored media literacy concepts and analysis questions as tools to teach students to examine promotional epitexts such as book trailers and other advertisements. With the skills to identify the anatomy of both print and video promotional texts, students from elementary to high school gain a better understanding of how advertisers target and persuade them as readers and consumers. Using book trailers or print advertisements as mentor texts, students can apply their knowledge and create promotional texts of their favorite books or self-published works.

Reflecting on Your Learning

What persuades you to want to read a book? Advertising? Word of mouth? Familiarity with the author's other works? Positive reviews? Think about this: movie adaptations are generally considered examples of extension epitext, but how might they also serve as promotional epitext?

References

Amazon. (n.d.). *Tyrant's tomb: The trials of Apollo, book four kindle edition.* https://www.amazon.com/dp/B07L4CDFPB/ref=cm_sw_em_r_mt _dp_U_R9USEbQQ5CVAN

Clow, K. E., & Baack, D. (2005). *Concise encyclopedia of advertising.* Philadelphia: Haworth Press.

Collins, S. (2008). *The hunger games.* New York: Scholastic Press.

Jacobs, L. (Director). (1994). *The magic school bus* [Television series]. PBS.

National Association for Media Literacy Education. (n.d.). *Media literacy defined.* https://namle.net/publications/media-literacy-definitions

National Association for Media Literacy Education. (2010). *The core principles of media literacy education.* https://namle.net/publications/core -principles

National Association for Media Literacy Education. (2013). *Key questions to ask when analyzing media messages.* https://drive.google.com/open?id =0B8j2T8jHrlgCZ2Zta2hvWkF0dG8

Nowell, S. D. (2019). Commercials as social studies curriculum: Bridging content & media literacy. *Journal of Media Literacy Education, 11*(3): 91–97. https://doi.org/10.23860/JMLE-2019-11-3-9

Over, J. (Director). (2000). *Clifford the big red dog* [Television series]. PBS.

Riordan, R. (2005). *The lightning thief* (Percy Jackson and the Olympians, book 1). New York: Disney Hyperion.

Riordan, R. (2008). *The maze of bones* (The 39 clues, book 1). New York: Scholastic.

Riordan, R. (2016). *The hidden oracle* (The trials of Apollo, book 1). New York: Disney Hyperion.

Riordan, R. (2017). *The ship of the dead* (Magnus Chase and the gods of Asgard, book 3). New York: Disney Hyperion.

Riordan, R. (2019). *Tyrant's tomb* (The trials of Apollo, book 4). New York: Disney Hyperion.

Rowling, J. K. (1998). *Harry Potter and the sorcerer's stone*. New York: Scholastic.

Scholastic Asia. (2020). *About us*. https://scholastic.asia/en/about-us

Scholastic Canada. (2019, July 5). Every book in the wildly popular I Survived series, by Lauren Tarshis Author, tells the story [Facebook]. https://www.facebook.com/ScholasticCanada/photos/a.155922037485/10157295994587486/?type=3&theater

Simpson, J. (2017, August 25). Finding brand success in the digital world. *Forbes*. https://www.forbes.com/sites/forbesagencycouncil/2017/08/25/finding-brand-success-in-the-digital-world/#74d75ebc626e

Tarshis, L. (2010–2020). *I survived* [Book series]. New York: Scholastic.

Weinberger, A. (2016, February 3). Hey publishers, just stop making book trailers. *Mashable*. https://mashable.com/2016/02/03/book-trailers-stop

Wells, W., Burnett, J., & Moriarty, S. (2006). *Advertising: Principles and practice*. Melbourne, Australia: Pearson Prentice Hall.

Wickline, K. (2011). *Book report alternative: Creating reading excitement with book trailers*. ReadWriteThink. http://www.readwritethink.org/classroom-resources/lesson-plans/book-report-alternative-creating-c-30914.html

Epitext in the CTE Classroom

Embracing Audiovisual Technology and Film Classrooms as Spaces for Developing Literacy Skills

W. Kyle Jones

The only light illuminating the 32 iMac computer lab is the projection of a breaking news segment pulled from a YouTube channel. Sleek, red-tinted graphics swirl around the lower third of the screen as bold lettering announces an unfolding event in a local community with the news station's emblem emblazoned on the lower right corner. A practiced and measured voice speaks authoritatively as a serious-looking news anchor with sharp features looks directly into the camera out onto the audience. Abruptly, the image stops moving as Ms. Lang pauses the video and begins to point out details of the still image, asking if students notice how the news anchor is framed or where information about the news story is located. As students note their observations, Ms. Lang uses their responses to point out important vocabulary such as "lower third;" she reminds her students that this is a model of what their news segments should look like as well, and excitedly explains how this project is a culmination of everything they have learned up to this point about the studio, cameras, and control room.

*As each new clip is shown and discussed in the darkened room, the students'
interactions vary. Carmen (all names used are pseudonyms), sitting near the
front of the room, eagerly participates and provides feedback to Ms. Lang
with each pause and question. Deidra offers a connection to her understanding of ethos, recalling her previous learning of written argumentation. Ms.
Lang springboards into asking the class to recall their use of ethos, pathos,
and logos in their recent research papers, which prompts one student, Bao,
to question how rhetorical strategies "fit" with a news broadcast. Ms. Lang
lights up at the question and quickly models how ethos might translate from a
research paper to a "Breaking News" segment, pointing out how a producer
of one segment purposefully labeled the show's guest as a "Lead Strategist."
She asks Bao and others what kind of "weight" a lead strategist has versus
having the source of information be an unverified Twitter handle. Bao quickly
draws the conclusion Ms. Lang is seeking, connecting that a lead strategist
sounds authoritative whereas a random tweet from someone does not.*

*Lively dialogue continues as the teacher continues to show models and ask
questions. However, one student, Kara, sitting near the back of the room appears openly agitated. As opportunities to turn and talk to a peer arise, Kara
voices frustration to the student sitting next to her. Her frustration turns to
anger as she expresses "how dumb" the project is and rhetorically asks "Why
are we even doing this?" None of this is aired within earshot of Ms. Lang.*

*As the discussion about "Breaking News" segments draws to a close and
fluorescent light fills the computer lab again, Carmen, Deidra, Bao, and
most of their peers start the task of revisiting their recently completed research papers and translating them to a broadcast. Some students are slow
to start, or simply seem to go through the motions of opening their work on
a computer, while Kara, arms crossed, decides not to log in at all.*

Introduction

The acts of scriptwriting and storyboarding are forms of *epitext*—the
text that supports or surrounds the final text (Gross & Latham, 2017). For
these forms of epitext, the final text could be a film or broadcast. When
students are invited to engage in the creation of epitext, rather than only
consuming and analyzing it, they have an opportunity to develop previously unexplored or underdeveloped literacy skills where—in the case of
audiovisual technology and film—dialogue, camera positioning, expression, and imagery become critical considerations for a final film (or text).

> We view these literacy
> skills as critical to be both
> consumers and creators
> of information.

In turn, this literacy skill development may
be influenced by the level of agency—the
"socioculturally mediated capacity to act"
(Ahearn, 2001, p. 112)—students feel em-
powered to enact or the level of access they
have to participate in the creation of these
epitextual elements.

In this study, students, both individually and in small, informal teams, created research papers; rundowns, which are two-column scripts used in broadcast filming; and a studio broadcast that were shared with and critiqued by the entire class. Before beginning this study, students were exposed to and had experience with some storyboarding and scriptwriting in their combination English language arts (ELA) and Audio Visual Technology and Film (AVTF) classroom.

The exploration and use of epitext in a Career and Technical Education (CTE) classroom such as AVTF serves multiple instructional purposes. First, it directly supports ELA standards focused on argumentative, expository, and narrative writing and writing revision. Second, it directly supports employability skills and literacy standards in CTE curricula. Third, it welcomes students to simulate real-world processes and transmedia navigation (Jenkins et al., 2009) while welcoming student agency.

This chapter explores the consumption and creation of epitext in the AVTF classroom as a means to welcome student agency and participation in authentic literacy practices.

Statement of the Issue to Be Considered

The CTE classroom is an overlooked space for students to develop meaningful and authentic literacy practices. An AVTF classroom is a particularly rich space for students to explore, take up, and create multimodal text, especially as it relates to drafting authentic texts such as storyboards and scripts that act as epitext for a final film or broadcast.

ELA teachers may struggle to provide authentic writing opportunities for students where their writing has professional applications or simulates those applications. In some cases, ELA teachers may even ignore the opportunity to open their classrooms to such authentic writing practices. An AVTF classroom welcomes the application of writing for authentic products such as scripts, rundowns, storyboards, and film reviews. When designed with intention, the curriculum of an AVTF class can provide opportunities to have students write fiction and nonfiction in a variety of styles,

> Allowing learners opportunities to create in a variety of modes and genres stimulates greater motivation and engagement. See Chapter 13, where Hunt discusses writing with robots as another example.

including writing arguments, expositions, and narratives, which are all common and expected writing styles in the ELA curriculum.

In addition, student participation and the agency students feel from writing, encountering, and using modes of epitext could become more apparent and authentic as well. Because the AVTF classroom is a space that welcomes the creation and use of epitext, examining that creation and use in that same classroom may illuminate important implications for student agency and participation as it relates to engaging in more meaningful and authentic literacy practices (Jenkins et al., 2009).

How the Work Is Situated in Epitext and Epitextual Framework

The specific functions of epitext are discussed at length in the Introduction to this book, p. ix.

What types of epitext do you make available to learners?

In Witte, Latham, and Gross's (2019) edited collection considering literacy engagement using peritextual analysis, Gross proposes that the next logical step beyond the Peritextual Literacy Framework (PLF) is "to explore the functions of epitext and how it influences motivation to read, critical thinking about works, and the interpretation and evaluation of works" (p. 11). This study captured students' production as epitext (rather than evaluating pre-existing epitext) and investigated what the potential effects of this work on student participation and agency might be. Witte, Latham, and Gross provide examples of production as epitext, such as drafts, outlines, and storyboards, to name a few. Students produced research drafts and two-column rundown scripts, all of which acted as epitext for their final newscast production. Additionally, students provided each other less formal feedback throughout their research and scriptwriting process, which might be argued to fit within epitextual analysis as well.

As noted later in the practical methods section, the classroom teacher provided students choice in their research topic and previewed breaking news segments for students to model the style and components of the production students were required to create. In this regard, the inspiration for the students' work came from topics they cared about or saw as important to their lives; they then expressed their stance on these topics across mediums.

Review of Relevant Literature

Gross (Witte, Latham, & Gross, 2019) explains that elements outside a text that may influence perceptions of a text and "mediate a reader's engagement with a work" (p. 4) are considered epitext. This implies that individuals may more often than not be passive consumers of such text—that the text influences an individual rather than an individual affecting the text. Gross and Latham (2017) argue that the exploration and analysis of either form of paratext—peritext or epitext—supports students' development of critical thinking skills. Here, a value is placed on the evaluation of text that exists. This study emphasized exploration and analysis of epitext through the production of epitext rather than the consumption of it, with the explicit purpose of encouraging student agency and active participation in such work.

When students participate in production of text rather than only consuming it, they have an opportunity to figure themselves in new social worlds where the "worlds are not pre-established, static entities, but rather are constructed by their members given their particular knowledge, interests, beliefs, and goals" (Beach, Johnston, & Thein, 2015, p. 120). In the case of epitext production, students' sense of agency may be influenced by their knowledge, interests, beliefs, and goals as they connect to the purpose of such text. Generating epitext provides a potential avenue for students to express their knowledge and interests, which in turn may create what Kelley (Jenkins et al., 2013, p. 70) calls an "intimacy and familiarity" with a text that leads to "recognizing certain patterns, images, or repetitions of thematic consequence" in their own creations.

Jenkins et al. (2013) point to simulations as compelling representations of knowledge for students, which engage them to make more discoveries and thus motivate students to move back and forth across complex transmedia. The creation of epitext can act as a simulation for applications to literacy practices across multiple mediums. For instance, the development of a storyboard visually mimics the frames and shots of a final film, simulating what will be. The storyboard is in time transposed into a new medium, but not before the storyboard simulates the vision of that new medium. Additionally, Jenkins et al. argue that as text and media have changed, an important part of participating in modern literacy practices is the evaluation of information, not only by using logic, but also by understanding how different mediums and communities operate. For example, moving the information captured in a research paper from that traditional form to a film medium requires a student to understand the innate differences in both mediums.

Finally, Clinton, Jenkins, and McWilliams (2015) concede that "to participate meaningfully, young people needed to be able to read and write; they needed to know how to connect their contemporary experiences to a much older tradition" (p. 5); however, they simultaneously argue that current education structures in the United States promote skills that are part of an outdated world. The implication is that students lose an opportunity to participate in meaningful ways when transmedia skills are not married to the tradition of reading a book or writing an essay. Epitext uniquely connects the old with the new, as most texts have forms of epitext surrounding them, including newer mediums and media outlets.

This chapter is meant to start a dialogue on the use of and place for engaging in creating epitext as a means to promote student participation across mediums and welcome their agency in the process.

Context

The author of this piece is a teacher researcher who currently serves in a support role for CTE teachers. He observed an AVTF and 11th-grade ELA combination classroom over a series of three months as a research and transmedia project was initiated, planned, and executed. The AVTF space included a dedicated computer lab with an adjacent control room and broadcast studio. The course, which was in its second year of existence, was designed by the AVTF teacher, Ms. Lang, who had also been an ELA teacher. This study was conducted at a high school located in the suburbs of a metropolitan area in the southeastern United States. The school of nearly 2,800 students was diverse. Demographically, the student body was approximately 16% Caucasian, 34% Latino, 30% Black, 16% Asian, and 4% Multiracial, with a free and reduced lunch rate just above 60%. The study included 18 11th-grade students who were participating in the AVTF and 11th-grade ELA combination course, with most students being considered on-level academically. The makeup of the class mirrored the school's racial profile and was nearly 40% male and 60% female. The students discussed were a small sample of the entire participant group and included one Black, female student, Deidra; an Asian, male student, Bao; a White, female student, Carmen; and a self-identified multiracial, female student, Kara. (All names are pseudonyms to protect the identities of the students and teacher.)

Practical Methods

Over the course of two months, students in Ms. Lang's AVTF classroom conducted research on a current event of their choice, and then wrote a research paper that was transformed into a rundown script and a mock newscast. At each stage of production, student artifacts were collected and four students—Deidra, Bao, Carmen, and Kara—participated in before-and-after- semi-structured interviews. All students in the class used peer and teacher critiques to engage in the work of revising their research papers and their approach to transforming their text into a broadcast. In addition to the reviews of student-produced epitext before filming, students critiqued and reviewed final film products in order to reflect on the impact of their stories on an audience and considered their own levels of participation.

> Participating in peer critique is an important skill for learners to experience. How do you model and mentor peer critique in your classroom or library?

The initial research papers focused on current events, with the distinct purpose of having students apply their knowledge and understanding of argumentation using a problem-and-solution format. The instructions for the paper provided a specific formula that students were to follow, including leading with an anecdote, transitioning to an introduction of a problem with a thesis that provided a possible solution, followed by descriptions of the problem and potential solution, and concluding with a justification for the solution that was crafted with the intent to persuade a "reader" to agree to the solution. The autonomy students had to choose a topic of their own interest facilitated a sense of agency for students with varying interests and beliefs. This was seen in the range of topics chosen. In the cases of Deidra, Bao, Carmen, and Kara, subjects ranged from police brutality to climate change to the effects of social media on developing brains. Students then took their research papers and converted them into two-column scripts, which are often referred to as *rundowns* in news broadcasting. These were the core epitexts that students developed; doing so required them to transform their traditional essays into small blocks of essential information to establish their arguments.

Bao researched climate change. In his research paper (Figure 10-1), he argued that lack of care and attention is the culprit for climate change and proposed that the best solution is tighter regulations on corporations. As Bao transformed his research paper into a rundown, his solution to combating climate change shifted. The rundown script (Figure 10-2) did not have the newscast decry the lack of regulation or attempt to rally others to press for regulation; rather, the script's dialogue focused on the effects of climate change with a general plea for the public to pay since this limits a lot of their previously held freedom that they have exploited. These laws would be enforced with a new agency, called the Earth Defense Force, named for the defense of the planet and its environment. This agency would be allowed police powers on par with, if not better than Interpol, and would conduct routine check ups on large corporations on a quarterly basis. Of course, they would be under strict regulation of the UN to prevent corruption of any sort from taking place. The downside to having such a big force is the monetary cost of running such a large police force, and paying each of the officers would amount to a high total as well.

Figure 10-1: Excerpt of Bao's research paper.

Green New Deal I think? It sets limits on the causes of climate change and promotes a healthier lifestyle for all. **Bao:** Nice. Back to you, Dee. ->	**Stare into camera** **Back in studio**
Bao: Just to reiterate, the Green New Deal is a deal set up by Rep. Ocasio-Cortez as a set of guidelines to improve the US as a whole. It's foundation was based off of the New Deal set forth by President Roosevelt during the Great Depression, and it seeks to replace all fossil fuels with clean, renewable source of energy, and insure jobs across the country. Other lawmakers still hold to the belief that it's too hard and very unrealistic to pull	

Figure 10-2: Excerpt of Bao's run-down script.

> How do you introduce the importance of tone and audience with learners? Why are they important to determine?

attention to the potential disastrous results. Bao revealed that he had intended to make his newscast "more lighthearted" and funny, but upon noticing others (like Deidra) also writing humorous dialogue into their scripts on serious subjects, he changed course, especially when he overheard Ms. Lang try to redirect other students from turning their research into a funny video opportunity.

The remix of Bao's and Diedra's research papers, which had a serious tone, into scripts intentionally written to showcase humor may have been a way to process serious topics. However, Bao explained:

> I thought humor would make [climate change] more interesting, and people would pay attention to it more because obviously people pay attention to stuff that is funny and not serious. So I thought maybe if I put a humorous spin on it that maybe more people would pay attention to it and be more aware of this issue and overall it would just be more entertaining. (Bao interview, May 13, 2019)

In Bao's view, the purpose of the remix of his research paper was to increase entertainment value in hopes of being more memorable. He expressed that he did not believe his peers would remember a serious broadcast about climate change. He reflected, "I wish there was more content in [my broadcast]. I mean, if you watched it now, I don't think [someone] would be unhappy with it, but I don't think they would be particularly pleased with it either" (Bao interview, May 13, 2019). When asked about his participation in the project, he explained that his lack of content had to do with his willingness to help his classmates with their projects. He felt compelled to help whenever asked, especially with the technical aspects of filming and running the broadcast booth.

Deidra, however, did not feel the same pull to help her classmates as she struggled to complete her own work. Due to a family emergency, her own filming and editing were delayed. Her background as an actor stimulated several classmates to request that she star in their own broadcasts, which she turned down in order to finish her own. When asked about her interactions with her peers, she expressed, "When it comes to grades we are all selfish in our own way" (Deidra interview, May 17, 2019). Her subject choice—police brutality—also played a role in her detachment from her peers. Deidra felt the subject was close to her as a young, Black woman, so when it came time to transform her serious and direct approach to her research paper (Figure 10-3) into a rundown (Figure 10-4), she found herself moving between humor and seriousness to navigate a sensitive topic. Ms. Lang directed Deidra to focus on the humorous tone in her script and broadcast, which Deidra claimed was helpful; she was grateful for the opportunity to express herself but present the topic in a way that she felt diffused the natural tension in the topic. Although Deidra expressed that she did not feel her final broadcast was well made, she did express her happiness with what she learned behind the camera:

> The project brought out more of my acting perspective and director perspective . . . I'm mostly known for acting so it brought up these aspects of how to be kind of bossy and know how to edit. All these things that I hadn't really thought of before. (Deidra interview, May 17, 2019)

What is police brutality? Louise I. Gerdes explained it best in his book "Police Brutality" saying that. "Police brutality is unruly, unjustified and used way too frequently". Rodney King, Stephon Clark, Trayvon Martin, Philando Castile and so many more people have been victims of this. Police Brutality is an issue effects victims of every race, and this problem will best be solved by better training to police officers. The definition of Police Brutality "The use of too much and unnecessary force by police when dealing with civilians". This has been a problem and has been growing even before the incident of Rodney King, in the late 1970s. King

Figure 10-3: Excerpt of Deidra's research paper.

Script:	
	IN the studio
Byline: Brought to you by your favorite anchor Deidra	it starts with music and insight news pops up and then it has my name as the by line and says anchor pans to me HS powerball ad transition and i'm standing has byline jacque damatay and background
Gooooood Mooooorning, I'm Deidra it is (say time and date) and this is goofy goofy news **Precis:** Coming up we will be talking about how that dang police is always using their weapons and change it. Also, Jack will be hitting you with the weather forecast all coming up on Insight News. Ad: HS Powerball number 6996 Jaque **Main Script:** Deidra reporter DJ reporting from outside of 400 where she is interviewing	Transitions back to the studio and the anchor is talking Outside of the 400 I am in the middle of K and L and about to interview them

Figure 10-4: Excerpt of Deidra's rundown script.

Deidra's exploration of film production was likely heightened by her development of epitext, as she explained that she had not realized how much work went into taking information and distilling it into a script that then has to be physically produced. Deidra saw the rundown—the primary epitext—as the bridge to transfer from one medium to another.

While Carmen's final product (Figure 10-5) was the most polished of those produced in this class, she expressed frustration with the process of transforming her research paper into a rundown, citing the difficulty

from Ms. Lang's 11th grade Honors Language Arts classroom. V, how are you?	
V: Thanks for asking Carmen I'm good! I am here with E and K. They are both 11th grader who's grades have been slowly declining due to their daily use of technology. E, how many text messages would you say you send a day?	Screen transitions back to me talking Lower Thirds: Social Media and Technology has a negative impact on teenagers.
E: Last month I had 27,000 text messages so I'd say about 900 a day! V: Wow and did that have any effect on you?	Change camera angle to the left side while I turn the attention to V
E: Well my phone definitely plays a bad role on my homework and grades because it distracts me a lot. I could be reading a book or doing homework and when I receive a message I immediately have the urge to check it. After I reply I will check all my social media; then about 20 minutes later I will	Lower Thirds: V with K and E Medium shot of all 3 people Zoom in on E, solo shot. Lower Thirds: E speaking on the effects of Social Media and Technology Side angle with all three of them

Figure 10-5: Excerpt of Carmen's newscast.

of taking 12 pages of research and translating them into a shortened dialogue for a script. In evaluating her literacy skills, she was humble and honest, explaining, "I'm pretty average slash above average because I'm good at writing, although I hate doing it, but I just find it boring. It's just not something I prefer to do" (Carmen interview, March 20, 2019). Despite her claim of being an average writer and struggling to convert her research into a broadcast script, she appeared to excel at pulling her project together, and produced a well-shot and well-edited newscast. She admitted seeing a benefit of taking a large amount of information and being concise: "like making an elevator speech" when introducing oneself to a stranger. In this case, Carmen related her creation of epitext to the preparation one might do for a verbal pitch. She, much like Bao, spent time during the project helping other students complete their projects, running the broadcast control room for several of them. She felt a closeness to her peers and wanted to help when she could, and indicated that the flexibility given in the class from Ms. Lang welcomed her to explore interests and get to know her peers.

Kara's experience generating epitext was quite different from that of her peers. She was the student from the opening vignette who at times could be openly defiant about the work and assignments. Frequently

> Collaboration is an important component of a global society. Collaboration is also discussed in Chapter 3 in relation to *Maus* and *MetaMaus*.

Kara expressed her restlessness while in the class, lamenting, "I feel like the skills I am learning are not that useful to me" (Kara interview, March 20, 2019) and summed up her participation by stating, "I feel like I do what she says because that's how you get the grade" (Kara interview, May 17, 2019). She struggled to commit to completing her project despite an evident passion for the topic of police brutality, turning in most of her work late or incomplete. She expressed feeling a distinct disconnect between her ELA work and her AVTF work, but also said that she enjoyed the challenge the class provided and how it was designed to be student centered. Her creation of the rundown as epitext felt disingenuous to her, as she did not feel someone could grasp the seriousness of police brutality through a newscast, explaining, "It felt extremely impersonal" (Kara interview, May 17, 2019). However, she was quick to point to her classmates as a source of support and connection, exclaiming, "My classmates are probably the only reason that I finished [the project]" (Kara interview, May 17, 2019). At one point during the interviews, she revealed that she had dyslexia and ADHD, which may have contributed to the delays in her work, but Kara never identified those challenges as the reason for the late work or her disengagement, pointing instead to what she believed was unclear directions and feedback.

Conclusion

When students create epitext rather than consume or analyze it, they have an opportunity to own the process of moving text across mediums and connect to the various purposes of epitext. In this project, epitext was an authentic distillation of research into a script rundown, as part of an overall project in which students participated in remixing media and navigating transmedia (Jenkins et al., 2009).

Bao, Deidra, Carmen, and Kara's experiences all varied, as might be expected; however, they universally experienced the challenge of moving text across mediums and experiencing the role epitext plays in creation of new iterations of a text. Each student, excluding Deidra, celebrated their peers' role in completing projects and seeing their work to the end. There was an opportunity to adopt the creation of epitext and feel connected to and valued by their peers when students navigated the transmedia they had created. Additionally, each student expressed some sense of agency, whether that expression centered on topic selection, the tone of their rundowns, or opportunities to coordinate and connect with their peers to complete the project. The AVTF classroom naturally welcomed students to demonstrate employability skills required by business and industry, encouraging group communication and problem solving. The addition of the embedded ELA curriculum provided students the opportunity to apply argumentative and expository writing techniques. Several students expressed seeing value in remixing their research to create a rundown and newscast; however, the connection to a valued experience is not a given or universal.

The creation of epitext is only as useful as a teacher can structure its creation or use. All four students lamented being uncertain about or unclear on expectations while taking their research papers and converting them into two different mediums. The purpose of constructing epitext in this project may have been lost on many students. However, there is an opportunity to be explicit with the purpose of constructing epitext, so students can connect a sense of understanding of its purpose to the value of epitext.

Educators have an opportunity to enhance participation and agency in their classrooms when utilizing the creation of epitext, which can oftentimes be a strong, authentic literacy practice. The AVTF classroom can be a welcoming space to see this come to life. However, without explicit modeling of the connections made between the epitext and the primary text, students may never consciously see the value of or seek to replicate this kind of authentic literacy practice. Teachers wishing to promote the creation of epitext in their own classrooms should consider embedding the creation of epitext throughout a school year, being explicit in pointing out why the epitext is valuable and useful to students' literacy practices.

Reflecting on Your Learning

What opportunities do you have as a teacher or librarian to collaborate across the content areas? What approaches can discipline-specific educators use to provide reading, writing, and critical thinking strategies and opportunities for learners? What potential epitextual projects can you implement as a form of assessment?

References

Ahearn, L. M. (2001). Language and literacy. *Annual Review of Anthropology, 30*: 109–137.

Beach, R., Johnston, A., & Thein, A. H. (2015). *Identity-focused ELA teaching: A curriculum framework for diverse learners and contexts.* New York: Routledge.

Clinton, K., Jenkins, H., & McWilliams, J. (2015). New literacies in the age of participatory culture. In H. Jenkins, W. Kelley, J. McWilliams, & R. Pitts-Wiley (eds.), *Reading in a participatory culture: Remixing*

Moby-Dick in the English classroom (pp. 3–23). New York: Teachers College Press.

Gross, M., & Latham, D. (2017). The peritextual literacy framework: Using the functions of peritext to support critical thinking. *Library and Information Science Research, 39*(2): 116–123.

Jenkins, H., Kelley, W., Clinton, K., McWilliams, J., Pitts-Willey, R., & Reilly, E. (eds.) (2013). *Reading in a participatory culture: Remixing Moby-Dick in the English classroom.* New York: Teacher College Press.

Jenkins, H., Purushotma, R., Weigel, M., Clinton, K., & Robison, A. J. (2009). *Confronting the challenges of participatory culture: Media education for the 21st century.* Cambridge, MA: The MIT Press.

Witte, S., Latham, D., & Gross, M. (eds.) (2019). *Literacy engagement through peritextual analysis.* Chicago, IL: ALA Editions and the National Council of Teachers of English.

PART IV

Epitext and Digital Spaces

CHAPTER 11

Critically Exploring Video Games and Their Epitexts

"I Never Thought Like This Before"

Brady Nash

Introduction

While the notion that video games can be sites of learning has been around for quite some time, researchers have only begun to look seriously at the role of games in literacy education over the past two decades. During this time, literacy research has taken a decidedly digital turn (Mills, 2010), with scholars exploring a variety of multimodal texts (Cope & Kalantzis, 2009) and considering the ways in which digital literacies and those practiced outside of schools (Skerrett, 2012) might find a place within English classrooms. As part of this examination, scholars have turned their attention to the importance of literacy within video games, which can function as literate objects of study in multiple ways. Games are themselves literacies (Gee, 2007; Steinkuehler, 2010) and often contain rich narratives (Ostenson, 2013). Moreover, they serve as the focal point of a body of other, largely digital literacy practices (Consalvo,

2017) when students read and write about them, share strategies with each other, and create videos and other media in response to games.

Despite an emerging body of literature highlighting the potential value of games for literacy and learning, researchers still lack a full understanding of how games and the multitude of cultural texts that surround them can be utilized in classrooms (Beavis & O'Mara, 2010). To help teachers and scholars better develop such understandings, this chapter explores the ways in which the critical study of video games, supported by the analysis and creation of online epitexts, can help students engage with video games on a critical level, inspire multimodal composition, and allow for a wider variety of students to be successful in English classrooms.

The chapter draws primarily from a 12th-grade elective English course in which students critically explored video games as texts by reading, interpreting, and creating a variety of game-related epitexts—those that surround a central text and inform the way it is understood and interpreted (Genette, 1997). Such epitexts included videos from the Game Developer's Conference and the web series Game Maker's Toolkit (https://www.youtube.com/channel/UCqJ-Xo29CKyLTjn6z2XwYAw), blogs and essays, popular and critical reviews, and even a classroom visit from a game designer. Students also created their own epitexts, drawing on those they had studied as tools to think critically about games and guide their own compositions. Student-created texts included personal essays, reviews, videos, and analytical presentations about topics such as the representation of race and gender in sports games or the predatory economics of mobile games.

> Finding connections between students' in-school and out-of-school literacies is key for engagement and motivation.

The introduction of games and epitexts into a course housed in the English department was intended to support students in the critical analysis of games in an academic setting and allow students' out-of-school interests to have a place in the classroom. As one student remarked, "I was never good in English when we just did books, but I can get into this—I played video games all my life but I never thought like this about them."

Video games and epitexts, when thoughtfully incorporated into a classroom setting, can help students develop critical approaches not only to the literature that is the traditional purview of ELA classrooms, but to the texts they live with outside of the school building. By highlighting curriculum, instruction and student activity around games and their epitexts, this chapter is intended to contribute to an emerging body of scholarship that highlights the ways in which popular texts, intertextually linked with one another across a variety of media, can be incorporated into literacy curricula and pedagogy. It is also meant to serve as a resource for teachers, librarians and educators interested in practical ideas for developing units on both games and epitexts.

The Function of Epitexts in the Course

Students in the course drew on a variety of epitexts in their study of games. These included public epitexts, those related to the promotion and production of games (e.g., talks and interviews from game developers), as well as reception texts (e.g., reviews, essays, and videos). This collection of epitexts served three central purposes:

> More information about public epitexts is provided in the introduction to this book.

1. to help students develop a critical conception of video games as texts that could be analyzed critically,

2. to expand the discourse community in which students saw themselves participating, and

3. to serve as mentor texts for students as they created their own analytical epitexts.

Through exploring the varied meanings of games in the context of their cultural ecologies, students began to frame their experiences with games critically, much as they were regularly asked to do with more traditional literary texts in their ELA courses. The critical emphasis was crucial for helping students build on their extant knowledge and experiences; while every student in the course reported extensive experience playing video games and engaging with epitexts such as YouTube videos, walkthroughs, or consumer reviews, none reported thinking about their gaming experiences critically or engaging with epitexts that did so. Moreover, epitexts are always addressed to an audience and often are created in response to one another; their inclusion in the curriculum, then, served to situate analytical thinking about games within a discourse community beyond the classroom.

Literature Review

Video Games in the World and in Classrooms

As multimodal texts and other new literacies continue to gain attention in literacy and English education, scholars have increasingly turned their attention to the potential of video games in English classrooms (Abrams & Gerber, 2014). The games industry now brings in more money than the film industry (Shieber, 2019), and games have been identified as a frequent and powerful component of students' corpus of out-of-school literacies, with between 72 and 97% of teenagers reporting some engagement with video games (Lenhart, 2015). Ostenson (2013), taking both the popularity and complexity of video games into account, highlights their potential in classroom spaces:

> There's a place for a purposeful study of video games in today's English classroom because they represent some of the most important storytelling in the 21st century. This new medium is not only connected to our students' lives and interests but also represents our society's efforts to push the boundaries of storytelling in meaningful ways. (Ostenson, 2013, p. 71)

Indeed, researchers have highlighted the ability of games to promote critical thinking and creative design (Altura & Curwood, 2015), motivate students (Pelletier, 2005), encourage reading printed texts (Abrams & Gerber, 2014), and support multimodal literacy practices (Gee, 2007).

Video Games and Their Epitexts

While video game epitexts have existed for as long as video games themselves, epitexts have exploded in the age of the Internet. As with any cultural object, games are situated within social contexts, and these contexts are mediated through various literacy practices and objects—videos, walkthroughs, reviews, critical analyses, blog posts, etc.—which function as epitexts that help gamers create meaning from their experiences with games. Millions of people engage with and create videos, walkthroughs, game streams, analyses and other forms of text to share with others online. Twitch, for example, a popular game streaming site, now hosts more than 2.2 million streamers and over 15 million viewers per day (Twitch Advertising) while popular gaming sites featuring commentary and essays regularly record 10–20 million viewers a month (eBiz-MBA, 2020).

Researchers have studied the role of game reviews (Altura & Curwood, 2015), cheat sites (Fields and Kafai, 2010), online forums (Steinkuehler and Duncan, 2009), Let's Play videos (Burwell & Miller, 2016), and gaming blogs (Berger & McDougall, 2013) both in and outside schools. These studies have highlighted the complexity of students' interactions with epitexts, and the ways in which they support engagement with and understanding of games. Such texts can support a critical approach to games, taking "emphasis away from the—often mechanical—process of playing the game and focus[ing] on the contemplative, creative, imaginative and productive elements of digital gameplay" (Apperley & Beavis, 2011, p. 134). In classroom spaces, then, epitexts can facilitate the incorporation of video games by providing specific venues and forms for critical attention to games as cultural texts. Students can read critical essays about games, watch analytical videos, or create their own texts related to games. Such literate activity not only mediates critical attention to games themselves, but also creates opportunities for students to engage in literacy practices across various media and modes.

Despite the research that has been done about both video games and their textual ecosystems, information about how students understand games as cultural texts that communicate meaning across semiotic modes is lacking (Beavis & O'Mara, 2010). As Pelletier (2005) writes, "there has been little research into how young people interpret the semiotic principles at work in games and the kinds of social functions students aim to achieve in producing texts relating to games" (p. 40). The logistical difficulty of incorporating games in classroom settings, alongside the stigma associated with gaming, have limited the incorporation of games in classrooms and the body of pedagogical knowledge surrounding them (Burn, 2004; Perrotta, Featherstone, Aston, & Houghton, 2013). Teachers considering including games within English curricula have largely had to create pedagogies from scratch. In exploring the study of both video games and epitexts, then, this chapter is intended to support educators and researchers as they explore the ways in which these texts might function in classroom settings.

Context

This chapter draws from a semester-long senior elective course at a semi-urban high school in a southwestern city in the United States. The course, titled "Video Game Analysis," was situated within the school's English department and fulfilled one-third of students' senior humanities requirement for graduation. Students chose this course, along with two other trimester courses, from a list that included Latin American Studies, Modernism, and Contemporary Fiction. The course had a small enrollment with only 17 students, only 3 of which identified as female. The author of this piece, now a doctoral student and university instructor, was also the teacher of the course. Just over half of the students in the course had previously been enrolled in 10th grade English with the same teacher two years prior. This English course, while it included light multimodal elements, privileged the study of literature and other texts communicated through alphabetic print.

Incorporating Video Game Epitexts
Teaching a Video Game Analysis Course

> What other types of non-print texts can be read? How do you introduce the idea of reading non-print texts to students?

In the course, students "read" games together. The teacher utilized several in-class structures for this shared reading, including playing games in class, with students passing around a controller and commenting on the play, students playing games individually on phones or laptops, and students playing games at home on school-provided laptops. These game-playing activities were embedded in analytical discussions, supported through readings and videos regarding the design and meaning of games. In addition to "gaming journals," students created reflective memos, an analytical paper, a review of a game, and one multimodal analysis of a game.

In contrast to a focus on video games as primarily narrative texts (Ostenson, 2013), the course allowed students to explore games as experiential and cultural texts, hewing closer to two traditions less closely tied to narrative: reader response theory (Rosenblatt, 1994) and critical media literacy (Hobbs, 2011). Rather than analyzing video games as stories, as students might analyze a novel, the class looked at them first as experiences, asking questions such as: What was the experience of playing this game like? How did meaning arise through our interaction with it? Secondly, students analyzed games as cultural texts. Students looked at their structure and the ways in which the rules and mechanics of games convey messages about the world. This exploration included analysis of racial and gender representations, messages about violence and the military, and the ways in which gaming experiences were situated culturally.

Video games analysis does not come easily for students, however, and games can be difficult texts to analyze. While the students had learned to think about poetry, novels, and other printed texts through analytical frames, they had never been asked to do so with video games. They knew how to find a quotation from a book or to re-read a poem when asked to write a paper about it. How, though, could they analyze an interactive experience? How could they describe an experience that passes by with time and uses sound, visuals, text, and interaction to convey meaning? Video games contain the formal aspects of numerous forms of media in a single text, and thus, it can be difficult for students to know where to begin. There are, of course, potential answers to these questions, but students did not begin the semester with them. Rather, they took up these questions as challenges to explore throughout the semester.

Epitexts in the Course

To aid in this inquiry, students utilized a variety of epitexts, looking at the ways in which writers, video creators, and game makers themselves conceptualize meaning in games. These texts included videos of games being played, videos in which narrators analyzed games, lectures and discussion panels, critical and reflective essays on games, and game reviews. These texts served to inaugurate students into a more critical space in which the formal, cultural, and philosophical aspects of games were actively debated and discussed, and into which students could add their voice—agreeing, disagreeing, responding and questioning. Within an epitextual landscape, students did not have to construct a framework for analyzing games alone.

Creating a Critical Culture around Games

Epitextual exploration began by reading several articles philosophizing about the nature of games: Roger Ebert's now notorious 2010 essay, "Video Games Can Never Be Art," alongside two exploratory pieces questioning or defending the value of games as meaningful texts. These three texts were written in response to one another, thus highlighting the discursive nature of online epitexts. As the class discussed these philosophical texts about the nature of games, students began to argue with the authors through both discussion and writing. Though none reported having previously conceptualized games critically, the class largely came to the defense of games. Students drew on their own experiences with games, their experiences with literary texts in schools, and their experiences with art both inside and outside of formal spaces to conceptualize gaming experiences as akin to those with other, more traditionally valued artistic texts. In this way, the reading of critical essays about the nature of games, alongside an exploration of students' own engagement with games, created a space for students to take ownership of the concept of games as cultural texts worthy of critical attention.

Throughout the course, students continued to read critical essays to help situate games within critical frameworks. As students played games, they also read and discussed these pieces together to extend their understanding of particular games, much as one might read literary criticism. For example, alongside a playthrough and discussion of the free mobile game *Temple Run*, students read an essay critiquing the game (Nash, 2012), arguing that it functioned as a form of capitalist productivity that simulated work for those unable to enjoy leisure. Students also found critical essays about games that they had played on their own, bringing them to class and writing about them in their gaming journals. In these ways, texts that functioned primarily through print (though most included images as well) served to infuse a sense of criticality into students' engagement with games, both those the class studied together and those that students played on their own time.

Game Analysis Through Video

Such critical texts were not limited to one mode or one purpose, however. Alongside written pieces, students also drew on video epitexts as sources of critical analysis. Alongside a playthrough of that game company's *Journey* (2012), students watched game designer Jenova Chen's speech "Emotion Oriented Interactive Entertainment" (Variety, 2013) and discussed the ways in which interactivity mediates meaning making and interpretation in games.

> How might these epitexts help students better understand the original text *Journey*?

Students explored popular YouTube channels such as The Game Maker's Toolkit, which provides in-depth analysis of the way individual games function to convey particular messages or create emotional reactions from players. In these videos, a narrator provides analytical commentary of a game accompanied by video clips that highlight the aspects of the game discussed in the voiceover. In one class session, students viewed an analysis (Brown, 2015) of Ubisoft's *Farcry 2* (2008) in which the video maker highlighted the ways in which the limited health and ammunition of the protagonist, alongside the imagery of a war-torn state, functioned in tandem to create a sense of danger and urgency. In the class's discussion of the video, a major narrative and thematic point about the game emerged: that the White, Western protagonist operating in an African context was a villain rather than a hero. Here, students' interaction with the video highlighted how the game makers drew on the particular affordances of games to create both an experience and a meaningful text that included a critical message about global politics.

Video essays also helped the class tackle the problematic nature of gender stereotypes (Extra Credits, 2015) and racial representations (Science Plus, 2015) in games. Such videos present weighty issues in an entertaining frame, utilizing humor, animation, and clips from popular media to invite viewers into conversations on complex topics. Drawing on the reference list from the latter video, students also engaged in a reading inquiry into these issues, which some took up as topics for their final projects.

These videos served two curricular purposes, the first of which was to deepen critical exploration of the rhetorical function of games' mechanics as well as the cultural messages embedded within them. In this respect, students began attending more specifically to games as designed texts that create both intended and unintended messages and experiences. Second, by utilizing the affordances of video (most notably the mixing of voiceover analysis with game footage), these videos highlighted a form of multimodal textual analysis that students could draw upon in the creation of their own epitextual projects.

Exploring Epitexts: Students as Literacy Investigators

To explore epitexts more explicitly and with greater breadth, students conducted inquiry projects in which they explored their own engagement with the textual ecosystem surrounding games. Students first reflected on the texts that surrounded their game playing, rounding up different texts they could recall interacting with. Students shared walkthroughs, cheat sites, Reddit forums, consumer reviews, business reports, rumor reports, online trailers, Let's Play videos, printed guides, and artwork based on games. They then chose one text to explore in greater depth and share with the class, discussing the ways in which it supported their gaming experiences in functional, aesthetic, or critical ways. This project helped students to think more broadly about the notion of games as culturally situated, as they discussed real examples of gaming situated within broader textual and cultural systems. Later, a game developer even visited the course and discussed the ways in which the online conversation surrounding a game can affect both its development and reception, and its creators personally.

Creating Epitexts

Each of these aspects of the course helped students prepare for their final projects, in which they created two gaming epitexts. The first was a review of a game chosen by each individual student. The class spent two days reading gaming reviews, collaboratively creating a list called "Features of Effective Game Reviews" (Table 11-1) which then served to guide their own writing. Students applied a critical lens to these as well, noting the reviews' focus on purchasing decisions rather than meaning or aesthetic experience. As they wrote their own reviews, students chose to adopt a more critical stance to the games they wrote about, approaching them more as artistic texts than as consumer products.

For their reviews, most students chose games they were familiar with, and many focused on particular topics within games. Topics included

Table 11-1: Students' List: Features of Effective Video Game Reviews

- Describes the gameplay
- Describes the narrative of the game
- Provides context—when it came out, what else was going on with games at the time?
- Gives personal information about the author and a personal take on the game
- Makes you feel like you know the author a little
- Discusses target audience—who would enjoy the game?
- Analyzes the game—is there meaning or a message?
- Interesting to read, even if you don't know the game

the portrayal of Black athletes in the football simulator *NFL Street* (EA Tiburon, 2004), the use of microtransactions in *Destiny* (Bungie, 2014), and the ways in which the independent role-playing game *Undertale* (Fox, 2015) uses humor and game mechanics to create a commentary on video game violence.

Students built upon their written work in the form of analytical videos surrounding games. Here, students worked to overcome the difficulty of drawing specific evidence from a text that is interactive by utilizing video or presentation software to "quote" from games visually. They recorded a voiceover, and then used screen captures of their own gaming experience as the visual text to accompany their words. Here, students used multi-modal elements (images and video) to take excerpts from the text just as they might include a paragraph from a novel in a paper or on a slide in a PowerPoint. Although they were still developing as video creators, students were starting to create multimodal analytical texts that could, if they chose, be shared with the world. Some students took up this invitation, joining the community of epitextual creators by posting their work online.

Discussion

Across activities, video game epitexts served several functions:

1. to help students think about video games as artistic texts worthy of critical attention,

2. to situate these forms of critical engagement within a broader discourse community, and

3. to serve as mentor texts for the creation of their own epitexts.

The first element could be subdivided into parts, as students analyzed the meaning potential of games in general, the rhetorical functioning of specific games, and their own experiences with games. Epitexts supported this critical attention in two ways: they provided analytical content regarding specific games, while also serving as models for the ways in which critical game analysis could occur.

Even though students interact with a variety of multimedia texts outside of schools, they rarely encounter models for critical treatment of these texts in English classrooms. By introducing epitexts culled from a community of thoughtful and critical game players, students could see the ways in which they might come to treat video games as texts worthy of critical attention and make connections across modalities. This shift mirrors Ostenson's contention that "once the students begin to see the unique affordances of video games, they are on the path to becoming more critical about the ways media work in their lives" (2013, p. 76). This shift, which was apparent in students' in-class activity, was also mirrored in students' reflections and end-of-course projects.

Epitexts, like any texts, do not exist in isolation. By engaging with them, students were engaging with communities who treated games seriously and shared their thoughts online via a variety of literate practices. Learning does not occur in a vacuum; rather, it is embedded within

> Nash highlights the critical point of the interconnectedness of all texts.

social contexts and communities in which learners participate (Gee, 2015). Bringing epitexts into the classroom helped students situate their critical activity within larger cultural discourse communities beyond the classroom. After the course ended, students interested in extending their engagement with games knew where to look to add their own contributions or to continue engaging with games socially and critically.

Moreover, by exploring their own engagement with both games and epitexts, students attended to the richness of their own existing literacies (Skerrett, 2012). Not only is their gaming itself a form of literacy (Gee, 2007), but all of them also had experience with a variety of other literacies related to their gaming practices. Through the critical attention they paid to games, the inquiries they conducted, and the work they created, students built upon these foundations an explicitly critical framework for understanding games. However, critical engagement with media does not end with the semester. Students can continue to apply the critical frameworks they have developed through their gaming habits and online engagement. Or, as Robbie told me, "I don't think I'll ever look at a game the same way again."

References

Abrams, S. S., & Gerber, H. R. (2014). Cross-literate digital connections: Contemporary frames for meaning making. *English Journal, 103*(4): 18–24.

Altura, G. J., & Curwood, J. S. (2015). Hitting restart: Learning and gaming in an Australian classroom. *Journal of Adolescent & Adult Literacy, 59*(1): 25–27.

Apperley, T., & Beavis, C. (2011). Literacy into action: Digital games as action and text in the English and literacy classroom. *Pedagogies: An International Journal, 6*(2): 130–143.

Beavis, C., & O'Mara, J. (2010). Computer games—pushing at the boundaries of literacy. *Australian Journal of Language and Literacy, 33*(1): 65–76.

Berger, R., & McDougall, J. (2013). Reading videogames as (authorless) literature. *Literacy, 47*(3): 142–149. https://doi.org/10.1111/lit.12004

Burn, A. (2004). From *The Tempest* to *Tomb Raider*: Computer games in English, media and drama. *English Drama Media*: 19–25.

Burwell, C., & Miller, T. (2016). Let's play: Exploring literacy practices in an emerging videogame paratext. *E-Learning and Digital Media, 13*(3–4): 109–125. https://doi.org/10.1177/2042753016677858

Consalvo, M. (2017). When paratexts become texts: De-centering the game-as-text. *Critical Studies in Media Communication, 34*(2): 177–183.

Cope, B., & Kalantzis, M. (2009). "Multiliteracies": New literacies, new learning. *Pedagogies: An International Journal, 4*(3): 164–195.

Ebert, R. (2010). Video games can never be art. *The Chicago Sun Times*. https://www.rogerebert.com/rogers-journal/video-games-can-never-be-art

eBiz-MBA. (2020, February). Top 15 best video game websites. http://www.ebizmba.com/articles/video-game-websites

Fields, D., & Kafai, Y. (2010). "Stealing from grandma" or generating cultural knowledge?: Contestations and effects of cheating in a tween virtual world. *Games and Culture, 5*(1): 64–87.

Gee, J. (2007). *What videogames have to teach us about learning and literacy*. New York: Palgrave MacMillan.

Gee, J. (2015). *Social linguistics and literacies: Ideology in discourses*. New York: Routledge.

Gennette, G. (1997). *Paratexts: Thresholds of interpretation* (J. E. Lewin, trans.). Cambridge, UK: Cambridge University Press.

Hobbs, R. (2011). *Digital and media literacy: Connecting culture and classroom*. Thousand Oaks, CA: Corwin Press.

Lenhart, A. (2015, August 6). Teens, technology and friendships. *Pew Research Center*. https://www.pewinternet.org/2015/08/06/teens-technology-and -friendships

Mills, K. A. (2010). A review of the "digital turn" in the New Literacy Studies. *Review of Educational Research, 80*(2): 246–271.

Ostenson, J. (2013). Exploring the boundaries of narrative: Video games in the English classroom. *English Journal, 102*(6): 71–78.

Pelletier, C. (2005). The uses of literacy in studying computer games: Comparing students' oral and visual representation of games. *English Teaching: Practice & Critique, 4*(1): 40–59.

Perrotta, C., Featherstone, G., Aston, H., & Houghton, E. (2013). *Game-based learning: Latest evidence and future directions*. Slough, UK: NFER.

Rosenblatt, L. (1994). *The reader, the text, the poem: The transactional theory of the literary work*. Carbondale: Southern Illinois University Press.

Shieber, J. (2019). Video game revenue tops $43 billion in 2018, an 18% jump from 2017. *Tech Crunch*. https://techcrunch.com/2019/01/22/videogame revenue-tops-43-billion-in-2018-an-18-jump-from-2017

Skerrett, A. (2012). "We hatched in this class": Repositioning of identity in and beyond a reading classroom. *The High School Journal, 95*(3): 62–75. https://doi.org/10.1353/hsj.2012.0008

Steinkuehler, C. (2010). Video games and digital literacies. *Journal of Adolescent & Adult Literacy, 54*(1): 61–63.

Steinkuehler, C., & Duncan, S. (2009). Scientific habits of mind in virtual worlds. *Journal of Science Education and Technology, 17*(6): 530–543.

Twitch Advertising: Audience. (n.d.). https://twitchadvertising.tv/audience

Video Games and Epitexts

Brown, M. [Game Maker's Toolkit]. (2015, January 5). Theme and mechanics in *Far Cry 2* and *Far Cry 4* [video file]. https://www.youtube.com /watch?v=Xm5myQWcJxc

Bungie. (2014). *Destiny* [video game]. Sunnyvale, CA: Activision.

EA Tiburon. (2004). *NFL street* [video game]. Redwood City, CA: Electronic Arts.

[Extra Credits]. (2015, February 18). No gendered mechanics—How genre stereotypes limit games and players [video file]. https://www.youtube .com/watch?v=ERR1F-zoTVg

Fox, T. (2015). *Undertale* [video game]. Toby Fox.

Nash, B. (2012, April 16). The anxious productivity of Temple Run. *Pop Matters*. https://www.popmatters.com/157304-the-anxious-productivity-of -temple-run-2495861891.html

[Science Plus]. (2015, September 28). How racist are your video games? [video file]. https://www.youtube.com/watch?v=yGyfcX2n4xY

thatgamecompany. (2012). *Journey* [video game]. Sony Interactive Entertainment.

Ubisoft Montreal. (2008). *Farcry 2* [video game]. Ubisoft.

[Variety]. (2013, February 8). Journey game creator Jenova Chen "Theories behind Journey" full keynote speech [video file]. https://www.youtube .com/watch?v=S684RQHzmGA

CHAPTER 12

Role-Playing as Epitextual Analysis

Evidence-Based Guidelines and Considerations for Facilitating Online Game-Based Role-Playing for Librarians and Teachers

Jonathan M. Hollister

Among U.S. teenagers aged 13–17 years old, 90% percent (83% of girls and 97% of boys) play video games of any kind on mobile devices, consoles, or computers (Anderson & Jiang, 2018). Video games are also popular with U.S. young adults between the ages of 18 and 29, with 60% (49% of women and 72% of men) playing games regularly (Brown, 2017). While around 77% of public libraries support gaming (Nicholson, 2009), few ALA-accredited library and information science (LIS) programs offer courses specifically focused on games and gaming (Hollister & Elkins, 2017). This suggests that librarians may be underprepared for including and using games and gaming in libraries. Exposure to games during their education helps pre-service librarians to understand the educational value and potential uses of games and reduce the negative stigma associated with games (Martin & Martinez, 2016). Playing games themselves may help educators and librarians to better understand how learning occurs through play (Moline, 2010). This chapter provides useful guidelines for librarians, school librarians, and teachers interested in promoting the development of epitextual and other critical literacy skills by leveraging the popularity and educational potential of online games and role-playing.

Statement of Issue to Be Considered

Epitextual analysis provides opportunities for readers to interact with texts and media they are already interested in and passionate about. As with books, a variety of epitextual elements are associated with online games. For example, alpha and beta testing versions of games could be considered production epitexts; game trailers and ads are promotion epitexts; videos or online streaming on Twitch.tv or YouTube are dissemination epitexts; game awards and reviews are reception epitexts; game expansions, player-modified adaptations of games, and fan fiction are extension epitexts; and quotes of game characters and players, comparison of games, and the influence of a game on its player community and other games can be considered referential epitexts. Game players and communities are not simply consumers of gaming-related epitexts: they actively create their own.

Types of epitext are discussed in the Introduction to this book.

This chapter explores one aspect of online games, role-playing, in which players use and create a variety of epitextual elements. Role-playing involves the creation of new characters and stories inspired by and expanded from a source material; typically, these are fictional works, such as fantasy- or science fiction-themed novels, movies, or games. Role-players interact with one another as their characters, living out stories, overcoming challenges, and adventuring within the world of the source's story, or one based on it. Intrinsically, the activities of role-players engage with and create multiple epitext types and utilize a variety of important literacy skills. As such, role-playing in online games may be leveraged to promote epitextual analysis skills, critical thinking, reading comprehension, and other literacy skills in a playful and enjoyable way.

This chapter also attempts to address the oft-grumbled perception that there is a disconnect between scholarly research and professional practice, related to the difficulty of applying theory or research findings to everyday work practices. Todd's (2015) framework for evidence-based practice encourages practitioners to use data and research to inform their workplace practices and make better decisions. In this vein, the guidelines and considerations here are derived from research on the information worlds and digital literacy practices of an online role-playing community in a massively multiplayer online role-playing game (MMORPG) called *WildStar* (Hollister, 2016). The guidelines and suggestions come from experienced role-players, with, of course, some interpretation and explanation to help translate and transfer their insights for practical use by librarians, school librarians, and teachers.

Review of the Relevant Literature

This literature review briefly discusses role-playing games, their use in library and information science, and the educational potential of online games.

Role-Playing in Games

In role-playing games, the role-playing aspect may refer either to the mechanical role a player fills (such as healing, protecting, or damaging others) or to activities and processes related to creating characters and engaging in interactive storytelling as said characters (Williams, Kennedy, & Moore, 2011). This chapter concerns the latter form of role-playing.

The characters and stories created by role-players are primarily based on and set within the story and content of the game itself (Hollister, 2016). However, concepts and ideas outside of the game's story may also be imported (Ilieva, 2013). If role-players choose a profession for their characters, they may consult sources about those jobs in the "real" world to make their characters more realistic and knowledgeable. As a role-player explains, "A piece of fiction only holds up so long as it's internally consistent. So, if I use anything else, I do everything in my power to conform to the rules of Carbine's [*WildStar*'s developers] Universe" (Hollister, 2016, p. 135). Continuing to describe the planning process for the character, a pirate, the role-player said: "I look at pirates, historically. How they worked, how they acted. And seeing how that fits with Carbine's pirates" (Hollister, 2016, p. 136). Role-players develop and use shared knowledge and cultural language to communicate and support role-playing activities in their community and game world (Ilieva, 2013). Communication and adherence to community-established rules are integral to and essential for maintaining a positive and enjoyable role-playing experience.

Use of Role-Playing and Games in LIS

Role-playing and games have been used as instructional tools for LIS students and practitioners. For example, Sheets (1998) employed role-playing to help train reference assistants, and Becnel and O'Shea (2013) used a role-playing game to teach public library administration practices in a virtual space. Librarians also curate and provide access to resources and reference services in virtual worlds such as *Second Life* (Mon, 2012).

Educational Potential of Online Games for Digital Literacies and 21st-Century Skills

The educational potential of games, even recreational ones, has been studied by researchers across several disciplines. Gee (2009, p. 4) argues that good games foster crucial skills needed success in the 21st century, including:

> embodied empathy for complex systems, "grit" (passion + persistence); playfulness that leads to innovation; design thinking; collaborations in which groups are smarter than the smartest person in the group; and real understanding that leads to problem solving and not just test passing.

Steinkuehler (2007) describes constellations of literacy practices in MMORPG players as they teach others; build in-game modifications or add-ons to manage data (also called *mods*, these are in-game applets allowing customization of the user interface); tell stories and create fan fiction; and establish norms and traditions. Martin and Steinkuehler (2010) note that players exhibit collective information literacy practices by collaborating when seeking and evaluating information, leveraging the skills of the group rather than one individual.

Martin (2011) argues that the sheer amount of game-related information necessitates information literacy skills to progress and succeed within a game. Galarneau and Zibit (2011) echo this notion, arguing that important 21st-century skills can be learned through playing online games. Role-players within *WildStar* demonstrated various digital literacy practices: information literacy in researching for their characters and stories; media literacy while evaluating media messages and creating media; and information communication technology literacy in using websites, forums, and wikis outside of the game to supplement and enhance role-playing (Hollister, 2019; Hollister, 2016). The dynamic nature of online games provides plentiful opportunities for learning and skills development, and role-playing within online games can provide another way to capitalize on these opportunities.

Online Game-Based Role-Playing as Epitextual Analysis

In this chapter, *online game-based role-playing* (RP) refers to the activities associated with creating and participating in communal stories as a unique character in an online game environment. During an RP event, role-players assume the identity of their characters and interact with other characters to perform various stories, ranging from daring adventures, to anthropological exhibitions, to social gatherings, and more. Role-playing in an online game world often occurs live or synchronously, though it can be done asynchronously outside of the game via forums, community websites, or social media. Role-playing is active in a wide variety of online games, including *World of Warcraft, Grand Theft Auto Online, RuneScape, Minecraft*, and more. The characters and stories created by role-players act as extensions of the primary "text" of the game. As such, role-playing most closely relates to the extension type of epitextual analysis.

Role-playing activities also relate to the referential and reception epitextual analyses. Characters and stories must adhere, more or less, to the norms and established content or lore of the game's official or canonical story. Story or lore information can come from the official "text" of the game itself, such as dialogue, graphics, cinematics, and audio; or from official sources outside of the game. Public authorial epitexts, such as social media posts and interviews with game developers, were often considered official sources of lore. Private epitexts, in the forms of correspondence, pre-texts and after-texts, such as developers' replies to role-players on social media and game patch notes (lists from game developers annotating game changes accompanying an update), also served as sources of lore information. This is where referential epitextual analysis comes into play. To justify an attribute of their character or aspect of their story, role-players often find, cite, and quote official lore information.

Within the role-playing community of *WildStar,* role-players often based their characters on official story or lore information produced by the game's narrative team (Hollister, 2016). Stories and events were frequently set in locations throughout the game world or acted out in player-customizable housing known as Skyplots, which could be designed to resemble homes, bars, laboratories, spaceships, or other settings. Within *WildStar,* two factions battled to gain control over Nexus, a long-lost, recently rediscovered planet hiding mysterious and powerful relics, creating a space-Western storyline infused with action and discovery (Carbine Studios, 2014). Given the science fiction and fantasy themes of the story and the attributes of the playable races, role-players created characters and stories that made sense within the world. Refugees, soldiers, scientists, business proprietors, pirates, spies, etc. were all fair game given the general setting and plotline.

Public and private epitexts from *WildStar's* narrative team were often used to fill in unknown or unclear aspects of the game's story. The role-playing community's process of determining what counts as official lore or not connects role-playing to the reception type of the epitextual analysis. Role-players not only review and provide feedback on the primary "text" of the game, they also review and critique their own epitexts: their characters and stories.

Considerations for the Pedagogical Applications of Role-Playing in Online Games

This section covers practical considerations for facilitating online game-based role-playing activities with children, young adults, or adults within classroom or library settings. Again, this chapter is based on my dissertation project (Hollister, 2016), an ethnographic study of the social information behaviors and digital literacy practices of role-players in *WildStar*. Data was collected, in part, through participant observation and engagement with the role-playing community, referring to those who created their own characters and participated in various role-playing events within *WildStar*. As such, the pedagogical applications and guidelines in this section are sourced from both the data and personal experiences.

Target Audience for Role-Playing Activities

Online game-based role-playing programs and activities are suitable for students and youth from grade 7 and up (ages 12 and up) and all adults. Depending on the types of stories and characters, permission or consent from the parents or guardians of pre-teen or teenage participants may be appropriate. Role-playing can be enjoyed at most ages as long as potential participants abide by the rules. Though no prior experience is needed, participants interested in gaming, literature, movies, creative writing, theater, comedic improvisation, or other creative hobbies may find their skills useful for role-playing. Some role-players are professional writers and role-play to have fun and to practice their writing skills (Hollister, 2016).

Making Space and Selecting Equipment for Role-Playing Activities

To facilitate online game-based role-playing in the library or classroom, the librarian or teacher should arrange access to gaming devices, such as gaming consoles or computers, or allow for participants to use their own devices. Some games support cross-platform compatibility, which allows users to play together using different devices.

Participants can log in from anywhere to role-play in an online game. Some online games allow local multiplayers to use a single device, and others are capable of being run on a local area network (LAN) or hosted on an online server for free or a small fee. If the event is held in a physical space, power and Internet infrastructure must have enough outlets and sufficient bandwidth, and there should be enough comfortable seating and tabletop space for device setup. If the event is held online, the host should ensure stable access to the game and administrative controls in case something goes wrong. Role-playing events can be lengthy, so organizers should plan accordingly, too; events in *WildStar* often lasted between one and three hours.

Role-playing in online games requires capable devices. The technical requirements needed to run each game vary, based on the type of game or supported devices. Game developers typically include hardware requirements with other information on their websites or within online retailer listings. Some game developers and hardware manufacturers have discount or grant programs for educational institutions, providing access for free or reduced prices. If access to a game is not possible, role-playing is possible using some of the technologies discussed in the next section, which are easily accessible via computers and various smart devices.

Selecting Games and Technologies that Support Role-Playing

A game's features may have a greater influence on the role-playing experience than its story. For instance, role-players liked the mysterious, sci-fi/fantasy themes of *WildStar's* storyline, but also cited the high level of character and housing customization and support for add-ons as reasons for joining that role-playing community. In the popular MMORPG *World of Warcraft* (*WoW*) (https://worldofwarcraft.com), role-players often install and use add-ons or mods to store and share role-playing information about their characters and stories. As seen in Figure 12-1, many role-players in *WoW* use the MyRolePlay (MRP) add-on (see https://www.curseforge.com/wow/addons/my-role-play), which can store various information about characters, such as physical attributes, race and cultural heritage, personality traits, description and history; and the players themselves, such as role-playing style, role-playing status indicating whether they are in-character or not, and other out-of-character information. Role-players using MRP can view each other's character profiles, which helps in keeping up with other players and facilitating dialogues and stories.

When selecting an online game to role-play within, pick a game that is appealing to the group of potential participants, allows for interaction and text communication, and provides sufficient character customization.

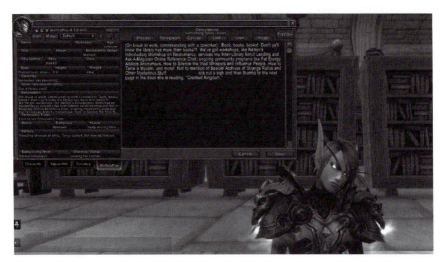

Figure 12-1: Screenshot of MyRolePlay Profile & Interface in *World of Warcraft.*

Role-playing can be facilitated in a wide variety of games, including many free ones as listed below.

Because participants will create their own stories and characters, games whose narratives include adventure, exploration, or mystery may provide accessible options for starting stories and a lot of inspiration. Online games such as MMORPGs; virtual worlds such as *Second Life* (https://secondlife.com); and sandbox games such as *Minecraft* (https://www.minecraft.net) or *Cube World* (https://cubeworld.com) provide worlds where players can do all sorts of activities, such as adventuring, battling, building, and crafting, alongside of or competing against other players. For mature players, online games such as *Grand Theft Auto Online* (https://www.rockstargames.com/GTAOnline) also provide opportunities for role-playing. Some MMORPGs, such as the *WoW: Starter Edition* (https://worldofwarcraft.com/en-us/start) and *Guild Wars 2* (https://account.arena.net/welcome), have free-to-play versions that provide access to core content that is sufficient to facilitate role-playing; game expansions often cost extra and are not necessary for role-playing. MMORPG .com maintains a large list of free-to-play online games (https://www.mmorpg.com/games-list/show/custom/id/1007). It is also unnecessary to have a maximum level character for role-playing; events are often held within in-game cities or areas accessible to low-level characters. Games allowing players to customize the race, gender, clothing, physical, and other attributes of their characters' in-game avatars are preferable.

Despite access to voice communication tools, role-players often conduct in-character activities entirely through text chat to maintain immersion. However, voice communication can be useful for quickly sharing out-of-character information. Discord (https://discordapp.com) is a free and easy-to-use cross-platform VOIP (voice over Internet protocol) program popular among gamers; users can create and host a free server for planning, facilitating, or conducting role-playing events using Discord. Planning for and conducting role-playing can be mediated using other online communication platforms, such as blogs, forums, and social media. Website and server hosting services, such as Enjin (https://www.enjin.com), provide free or low-cost solutions for a dedicated online space outside of the game.

Connecting with Library Resources

Nicholson (2010) argues that gaming programs are a great way to connect library resources with new and reluctant users. Creating and managing characters and their stories requires time and research, a process that can last anywhere from a few days to multiple weeks (Hollister, 2016). Character design involves determining appearance, background, personality, profession, and more. During initial planning meetings, librarians and teachers should introduce and show participants how to find or access books, programs, services, or other classroom or library resources that may be useful for prospective role-players when planning their characters and stories. For example, books on fiction writing or improvisation; thematically similar novels, games, or movies; author visits; or creative writing workshops can all be helpful for new role-players. Another example: if the character is a pilot, books about being a pilot or about a famous pilot may help the participant create a more realistic character.

Evidence-Based Guidelines for Facilitating Online Game-Based Role-Playing

The guidelines here are organized into three main sections based on categories of social norms or generally-agreed-upon rules identified in the study of online role-players: story and information management; character design; and community health (Hollister, 2016). These guidelines and tips will help facilitate an inclusive, enjoyable, and healthy role-playing experience.

Story and Information Management Guidelines

This section focuses on how to manage information related to role-playing activities both within and outside of the game.

Managing In-Game Role-Playing Information

Role-players in online games that support add-ons or mods often create or use mods to manage role-playing information. Within *WildStar*, role-players used an add-on called PDA (Personal Data Accessor) to store profiles about their characters, similar to MyRolePlay in *WoW*, described earlier. Creating or using add-ons can help players connect and stay organized.

Even without add-ons, role-players must manage in-character and out-of-character information during RP events. Role-players observed in *WildStar* used specific channels and symbols to denote different types of communication (Hollister, 2016). For example, role-players used private chat for out-of-character, person-to-person conversations, and local say, party, or custom emote chat channels for in-character role-playing. Using double parentheses (()) around a statement designated it as an out-of-character message ((my dissertation was too long)), and was used to make corrections or clarifications without switching chat channels (Hollister, 2016). Out-of-character communication occurred in parallel with in-character role-playing dialogue to guide the story, ask questions, and obtain consent. The role-playing group must designate where, when, and how to efficiently communicate in-character and out-of-character information.

Managing Outside-of-the-Game Role-Playing Information

A community website, wiki, or discussion board can provide a place for role-players to store their profiles, draft plots and get feedback, and participate in asynchronous role-play. An external space for storing role-playing information is especially important if the online game does not support add-ons.

Character Design Guidelines

This section focuses on rules and tips for creating engaging and interesting characters while avoiding common pitfalls.

Be Whoever You Want, Mostly

Created characters should make sense within the game world. As one role-player stated, "the most important information that all RPers [role-players] must research most deeply is the lore of the MMO itself. There's definitely no buts to it. Can't have people breaking lore and start making fairy princess vampire characters. @_@—" (Hollister, 2016, p. 138). However, if the selected game has lore to support fairy, princess, and/or vampire characters, or if the role-players agree to allow it, then it is permissible.

Do Not Be Yourself

Characters should be different from their players, their jobs, and their personalities. If they are too similar, players may take more offense to perceived slights or actions taken against their characters, resulting in unnecessarily hurt feelings. Though it is pretty much impossible to make characters completely dissimilar from their players (which is okay), participants should be encouraged to explore new identities.

Perfect People Not Allowed

Characters who are perfect, all-powerful, all-knowing, or too special are no fun for other role-players. As one role-player states (Hollister, 2016, pp. 98–99):

> [C]reating mary sues is also a RP stigma. As for what will happen when someone breaks one of these rules, it'll be really one complicated drama to diffuse. For example, if someone godmods or powerplay their characters, using as means to trample on other RPers' characters, it'll not be fun for others and downplaying their characters without any regard to the players' consent. Which is very disrespectful.

Thus, encourage participants to create realistic characters, complete with strengths, weaknesses, personality quirks, and challenges of their own.

Community Health Guidelines

This section focuses on insights to foster a positive and active role-playing community mindful of its members' well-being.

Role-Playing Requires Consent

Though most role-playing stories are improvised and performed live, role-players must be careful to respect the choices and preferences of other players. Because role-playing is a collaborative experience, role-players should check in with others to ask them if it is okay for their characters to interact in a certain way or for the story to turn in a new direction. Out-of-character communication is often used to obtain consent for potentially traumatic experiences, such as romance or violence. If a player wants their character to discriminate, flirt, touch, harm, or even kill another player's character, those actions require consent from the player behind the other character.

> Consent is central to maintaining respect among players and avoiding negative experiences.

Morally Grey Role-Playing Is Okay

Role-players create all sorts of identities and storylines, ranging from heroes to complicated anti-heroes to villains, who, variably, save or doom those they encounter. Building on the previous guideline, if a character is evil, their actions on or against other characters are only okay if the players involved communicate and consent to it. Role-players should be encouraged to identify topics and situations they are uncomfortable with in their in- and out-of-game character profiles, to help prevent uncomfortable and traumatic experiences. Problematic characters or stories involving discrimination, prejudice, abuse, coercion, or violence of any kind may have to be explicitly banned by the community to discourage negative role-playing experiences.

> Remember that in role-playing, issues of consent, and maintaining established rules always apply.

Keep In-Character and Out-of-Character Information Separate

The boundary between in-character and out-of-character interactions is critical for multiple reasons. If a role-player is too close to their characters, they risk having their real-life feelings hurt. Furthermore, conflicts between characters should be understood to be limited to the story—that is, they do not extend to the players in the real world.

The immersion of role-playing can be disrupted if out-of-character information leaks into in-character interactions. Characters should not be aware of information that their players know or discuss with others while out of character. If a character acts in a certain way because they know something they should not, it can disrupt the event by spoiling the fun and improvisational nature of role-playing.

Discuss, Post, and Enforce Role-Playing Rules

These guidelines should be discussed with the prospective participants and used to establish rules. An accessible community space outside of the game, as discussed earlier, should also be used to post and discuss the community's guidelines and rules. Organizers should set clear expectations and enforce community rules as needed.

Getting Started

Role-playing as a process is adaptive and flexible, allowing for multiple approaches ranging from light or casual role-playing to heavy, always-in-character role-playing. This means that teachers, librarians, and their groups of learners will need to determine an approach that works best for them. Additional resources in the appendix to this chapter and videos or streams on YouTube or Twitch.tv can provide helpful insights. Connecting with other librarians, teachers, staff members, or learners with gaming or role-playing experience may provide valuable information and assistance.

Before jumping right into role-playing activities, schedule initial planning and practice meetings with interested librarians, teachers, and learners. At the first meeting, the organizing librarian(s) or teacher(s) and potential participants can establish and clarify rules, and decide on the game, plotline, or themes upon which role-playing activities will be based. Organizers can then set up a community space or additional services and show participants how to find and use relevant epitexts and other resources to aid character and story development. The second meeting, and more as needed, can be used to review the rules, practice the role-playing process, and troubleshoot technology issues before fully fledged role-playing events are started. The organizing librarians and/or teachers are encouraged to get into character, too. Participants will begin to settle into their characters, stories, and the role-playing process through subsequent meetings. As the stories grow and plots thicken, there will be continuous opportunities to engage using epitextual analysis and other critical literacy skills.

Conclusion

Given the popularity of online games, availability of free-to-play or low-cost games, lower technical requirements, better performance-for-value devices, and broader device compatibility, incorporating online games into libraries and classrooms is much more feasible than it was in the past decade. Role-playing in online games has the potential to engage epitextual literacy skills and other skills critical for success in the 21st century. In the process of developing and enacting their characters and stories, role-players engage a wide variety of epitexts while also creating new epitexts to support their activities. Using the guidelines and resources in this chapter, librarians, teachers, and their communities can embark on a fun and safe role-playing adventure to worlds both known and unknown.

Reflecting on Your Learning

Do MMORPGs play a role in your work? How can MMORPGs increase critical thinking skills? How might the skills learned in MMORPGs transfer to other digital learning environments?

Acknowledgments

The data used to inform the guidelines and considerations discussed in this chapter were collected and analyzed as part of my dissertation project. A citation and links to the full dissertation are included in the reference list.

References

Anderson, M., & Jiang, J. (2018, May 31). *Teens, social media & technology 2018*. Retrieved from Pew Research Center website: http://www .pewinternet.org/2018/05/31/teens-social-media-technology-2018/

Becnel, K., & O'Shea, P. (2013). Teaching public library administration through epistemic gaming. *Journal of Education for Library and Information Science, 54*(4): 235–243.

Brown, A. (2017, September 11). *Younger men play video games, but so do a diverse group of other Americans.* Retrieved from Pew Research Center website: http://www.pewresearch.org/fact-tank/2017/09/11/younger -men-play-video-games-but-so-do-a-diverse-group-of-other-americans/

Carbine Studios. (2014). *WildStar* [computer game]. Retrieved from www .wildstar-online.com

Galarneau, L., & Zibit, M. (2011). Online games for 21st century skills. In *Gaming and simulation: Concepts, methodologies, tools, and applications* (pp. 1874–1900). Hershey, PA: Information Science Reference.

Gee, J. P. (2009). Games, learning, and 21st century survival skills. *Journal of Virtual Worlds Research, 2*(1): 3–9.

Hollister, J. M. (2016). *In- and out-of-character: The digital literacy practices and emergent information worlds of active role-players in a new massively multiplayer online role-playing game* (Doctoral dissertation). Retrieved from ProQuest Dissertations and Theses Global database (UMI No. 10120632). Retrieved from DigiNole website: http://fsu .digital.flvc.org/islandora/object/fsu%3A360374

Hollister, J. M. (2019). An ethnographic study on the digital literacy practices of role-players in a massively multiplayer online role-playing game. *Journal of the Korean Library and Information Science Society, 50*(4): 429–467.

Hollister, J. M., & Elkins, A. J. (2017). *Power up: Gaps in and opportunities for gaming in LIS curricula.* Poster presented at the 2017 ALISE Annual Conference, Atlanta, GA, January 17–20, 2017.

Ilieva, A. (2013). Cultural languages of role-playing. *International Journal of Role-Playing,* (4): 26–38. Retrieved from http://ijrp.subcultures.nl/

Martin, C. (2011). An information literacy perspective on learning and new media. *On the Horizon, 19*: 268–275. https://doi.org/10.1108/10748121111179394

Martin, C., & Martinez, R. (2016). Games in classroom and practice in library and information science education. *On the Horizon, 24*(1): 82–87. https://doi.org/10.1108/OTH-08-2015-0051

Martin, C., & Steinkuehler, C. (2010). Collective information literacy in massively multiplayer online games. *E-Learning and Digital Media, 7*(4): 355–365. https://doi.org/10.2304/elea.2010.7.4.355

Moline, T. (2010). Video games as digital learning resources: Implication for teacher-librarians and for researchers. *School Libraries Worldwide*, *16*(2): 1–15.

Mon, L. M. (2012). Professional avatars: Librarians and educators in virtual worlds. *Journal of Documentation*, *68*(3): 318–329.

Nicholson, S. (2009). Go back to start: Gathering baseline data about gaming in libraries. *Library Review*, *58*(3): 203–214.

Nicholson, S. (2010). *Everyone plays at the library: Creating great gaming experiences for all ages*. Medford, NJ: Information Today.

Sheets, J. (1998). Role-playing as a training tool for reference student assistants. *Reference Services Review*, *26*(1): 37–41.

Steinkuehler, C. (2007). Massively multiplayer online gaming as a constellation of literacy practices. *E-Learning*, *4*(3): 297–318.

Todd, R. J. (2015). Evidence-based practice and school libraries: Interconnections of evidence, advocacy, and actions. *Knowledge Quest*, *43*(3): 8–15.

Williams, D., Kennedy, T. L. M., & Moore, R. J. (2011). Behind the avatar: The patterns, practices, and functions of role playing in MMOs. *Games and Culture*, *6*(2): 171–200. https://doi.org/10.1177/1555412010364983

Appendix: Additional Resources

American Library Association Games & Gaming Round Table. (n.d.). *Games in libraries.* **https://games.ala.org**
This blog, produced by members of the Games and Gaming Round Table (GameRT) of the American Library Association, has a variety of useful resources and active discussions.

Dufferin. (2017). *Basic roleplaying guide for beginners.* **https://www.wow head.com/guide=2569/basic-roleplaying-guide-for-beginners**
A simple starter guide for role-playing in the MMORPG *World of Warcraft.*

Extremely Casual. (2017, July 14). *Role-playing—A beginner's guide* [video file]. **https://youtu.be/xMEMNPaMv9s**
A light-hearted YouTube seminar for new role-players in MMORPGs.

Inverse Genius. (n.d.). *Games in Schools and Libraries.* **http://www.inverse genius.com/games-in-schools-and-libraries**
A podcast and blog dedicated to using games in library and classroom settings.

Mojang. (2020). *Minecraft: Education edition.* **https://education.minecraft .net**
Minecraft for educational settings, complete with resources, support, and lesson plans.

Roleplay Headquarters. (2015, February 15). *RPing in MMOs: A beginner's guide [Introduction to Roleplay]* **[video file]. https://youtu.be /gPTeePcUsQw**
The first episode of an informative four-part series on role-playing in MMORPGs.

Twelves, K., Blankensop, M., Klein, M., & Warner, J. B. (n.d.). *Improv for gamers.* **http://www.improvforgamers.com**
Workshops and a book on how improvisational acting skills are useful for role-playing.

CHAPTER 13

Binary Texts Challenge Epitext

Robot Poems, or Poem Robots?

Katie Henry and Bud Hunt

A poem is not a ready-made object to which a reader is passively exposed. A poem is a happening, an event, in which the listener or reader draws on images and feelings and ideas stirred up by the words of the text; out of these is shaped the lived-through experience.

—Louise Rosenblatt (1980)

At the end of the three-hour workshop, a teacher lingered. During the workshop, Katie and Bud had learned that the teacher was a high school science teacher. Bud suspected he wanted to inquire about a particular model of robot to purchase from Katie, who, at the time, was the professional development manager for a robotics company.

Bud was mistaken.

The teacher, expecting to learn more about how to program robots, had found himself writing through some powerful memories. He wanted to know more about writing, and if his experience freewriting poems with us was normal.

"Does writing always make you feel this way?" he asked them both. Bud doesn't remember how he answered the teacher's question, but he knew that something special had just happened for the teacher: an experience that might lead to classroom change as he and Bud discussed ways to incorporate more writing into the teacher's high school science classroom. As the teacher had written, then composed, his ideas through words and robotics, he had rediscovered something precious about the world that he wanted his students to experience, too.

Bud and Katie think about that teacher's question often.

Let's Ada Lovelace This Thing

Many of the more interesting experiences of our professional careers have arisen out of happenstance moments, juxtapositions of ideas that create moments to look at what we know in new ways in order to discover that which we may *not* know. Such was the case when we found ourselves in conversation with a makerspace coordinator and a language arts teacher, both in California, in April 2018. The conversation was an attempt to explore possibilities for some professional development experiences for maker educators modeled on the summer institute experiences of local sites of the National Writing Project. As we discussed how we might create spaces for maker learning and language arts instruction to intersect, Kelly Matteri, the aforementioned language arts teacher, mentioned that she would like to "Ada Lovelace up" the integration of writing and maker work. She (or perhaps, looking back, it was us projecting) was frustrated with the pseudo-integration moments of many STEM or STEAM classrooms, and the ways in which the various subjects were too often clumsily shoehorned together to create Franken-experiences: unnatural moments where artificial domains, school-only domains, were made to make knowledge. From her idea, and our shared frustrations and sense of much room for improvement, our robot poem (or poem robot) workshops were born.

As we began to explore other places where multidisciplinary and multimodal composition was occurring, we returned to the story of Ada Lovelace, the daughter of Lord Byron, who was also a contemporary of, and by many accounts, collaborator with Charles Babbage, father of the Difference and Analytical Engines, seen by many as the precursor to modern computers. There is both the historical story and the popular version. The idea of Lady Lovelace, someone standing actively in both poetry and mathematics, is sufficient for our purposes.

Lovelace, operating from her "poetic science" lens, explored what practical uses such computational machines might be put to. Due to her poetical imagination, she saw potential in what the analytical engine might be able to do. We see similar opportunities in complicating what counts as composition in the makerspace and the language arts classroom.

Drawing on our experiences with open-source robotics tools and poetry instruction, we envisioned creating an experience where writing poetry would provide the foundation for thinking about the physical construction of robots. A *robot,* as defined by Katie, is a machine that can [at least] sense, think, and act.

Interested participants—specifically teachers as we originally envisioned the experience—would begin by writing poems with us, generated through the use of Taylor Mali's Metaphor Dice (http://metaphordice .com), a tool that at that time was being kickstarted into existence. The dice provide basic concepts that can be combined through rolls into metaphors that can help provide a freewriting prompt for poetry. After those prompts first came to life as written words on a notebook page or computer screen, we would then ask participants to bring them to life as physical substantiations of small robots. This was an opportunity to introduce the Hummingbird Bit (https://www.birdbraintechnologies .com/hummingbirdbit), an interface built by Birdbrain Technologies to extend the micro:bit, a small and inexpensive computer to teach computing concepts to students. The micro:bit (https://microbit.org/) is a popular entry-level physical computing tool: the $15 board contains a small screen, several sensors, and other input and output tools.

Robot Poems, or Poem Robots?

As our participants began to make their poems into small robots, we noticed something. We hoped it would happen, but we were surprised by how powerfully the poetry was transformed into a physical thing. And then the more interesting thing happened: the poets and makers returned to their words, making revisions based on what they learned and discovered as they crafted their robots. Then the poets returned to their robots, making revisions to them as well.

Two primary texts were created in the workshop that day, and in the versions we've run since: a poem and a robot. Both texts spoke to the other: robots revising poems revising robots. And vice versa.

This back-and-forth textual creation happened much faster than Katie sees in many of her robot experiences and Bud sees in writing workshops. Something about robot poems is contrapuntal, multiple melodies taking turns and creating polyphonic meaning for the participants expressed in their creations. As one composes into robots through words or into words through robots, the experience in both modalities is enriched as the texts speak to each other and to the other texts under construction within the classroom. Boundaries are blurred, compositional goals are broadened, and surprise abounds. Teachers who embrace these blurred lines might be creating richer interdisciplinary experiences for their students than those who are not.

Within the epitext literacy framework, there is an implicit assumption that one text is the primary focus of study. All other texts are supporting, or refining, or evaluating, or otherwise acting on the primary text. In some ways this is the case in our workshops, as we often begin by writing poems before constructing robots. But by the conclusion of our robot poem experiences, there was not a single text that drove the show. There were two. The poems and robots, as Rosenblatt outlines earlier, were happening, and they were happening together.

> What kind of epitext exists that points to robots? What functions does that epitext fulfill?

In this chapter, we further explore how these robot poems (poem robots) serve as dual primary textual experiences, or at least as competing primary texts, and how they take turns as texts that influence each other in a variety of ways as seen through the functions of epitext.

Relevant Literature

Genette (1997, p. 344) locates epitext as "anything outside the book," though he also allows that epitext can, if added to the text it discusses or describes, become peritext. He also describes the public epitext and the private epitext, referencing the original primary audiences for such work, and not necessarily the intended ones, describing an intimacy in the audience of the private (1997, p. 371). This recognition of complexity of audience in considering epitextual elements is worth a mention here, as the work we will later describe, though written in "public" (the context of the workshop or classroom), contains elements of privacy as emotional images and memories are accessed. The text of the poem becomes the text of the robot, and back again; notions of public, private, primary, and secondary all seem to swirl around the binary star of robot and poem that participants are experiencing in our workshops.

> What makes epitext public or private?

Emig's (1977) widely cited and widely argued case for writing as a tool for learning comes to mind as we explore what's occurring in the robot poem experience. Emig claims that "[w]riting serves learning uniquely because writing as process-and-product possesses a cluster of attributes that correspond uniquely to certain powerful learning strategies" (p. 122). Writing as a tool for thinking, not just modeling thinking, helps to situate written work as both evidence of learning and a process for learning. To return to the science teacher, writing can, when used well, feel "that way."

Writing, composition, or even "making" are all activities that serve the process and product cycle Emig describes. Drawing on Vygotskian ideas of learning as social activity, Smagorinsky (1995) has described meaning construction as the goal of learning, and has emphasized that different disciplines should consider "the historical values of the discipline and the consensus of participants" (p. 162) when it comes to considering the proper medium for meaning construction within a discipline. Using this idea to reconceptualize the role of writing as a tool for learning, writing more broadly becomes composition or construction. Learning, then, is making things with appropriate tools. The "historical values of the discipline" of robotics are very much up for discussion and debate at present; students and their teachers would strongly benefit from more attention to how robots are made. Nevertheless, an injection of poetry, of humanity itself, seems necessary to ensure better outcomes for society at large. STEM instruction, even with an occasional "A" for art dropped in from time to time, should not be solely about preparation for work or career. Robot poems, a complication of two disciplines, where language arts and computer science are in conversation at the point of individual meaning construction, seem a useful tool in this regard.

When Jenkins (2007) describes transmedia experiences and world building, he is generally referring to cross-platform storytelling of a fictional nature. The multiple texts across various modes result in a richer experience for readers. An individual creating a poem across multiple modes may well create a richer experience, too. Robot poems are a small multigenre moment, as Romano (2000) suggests, though robots are perhaps a further leap from the types of genres Romano describes.

Rosenblatt (1980) reminds us that reading is transactional: a reading of a text requires both the text and an active reader. But she also reminds us that reading for comprehension is not the only reason to approach text. There is an emotional component as well, one that is not secondary in importance. A reader approaches a text through multiple lenses, one efferent, the other aesthetic. Classrooms and those who facilitate them all too easily forget that, as she reminds us, "efferent and aesthetic reading are parallel" (p. 388), and young readers—in fact, all readers—should be able to come and go from sense making with logic and emotional response. Rosenblatt cautions teachers not to confuse the two, or overly privilege efferent readings, as they might harm the development of the aesthetic lens. She describes an "unfortunate pendulum swing" away from aesthetic reading that feels all too true today, some 40 years after she penned those lines. This swing, oft bemoaned from generation to generation as a societal rejection of the importance of the humanities, seems cyclical, as we continually rediscover ourselves and our stories through literature and poems. Might robot poems, and experiences like them that bridge traditionally viewed disparate disciplines, be a productive way to balance readerly lenses?

Composition is messy and multimodal and happens in lots of different ways.

Bringing Poems to Technologists and Technology to Poets

Although we have conducted our workshops in a variety of locations and as a portion of several different conferences, our largest audiences have been at technology-related conferences. In all cases, the basic format proceeds as described earlier. We outfit our workshop rooms with the necessary materials to construct robots (Table 13-1): specifically, a large collection of craft supplies and microcontrollers and accessories for participants to use in pairs or small groups (though often participants break off on their own to explore an idea or potential creation).

Table 13-1: Workshop Materials

Electronics	Craft supplies
Micro:bit and/or Hummingbird Bit Kit	hot glue Velcro dots masking tape
ChromebookLaptop or mobile device	reused cardboard packing material
	scissors hole punch box cutters cutting mat
	markers felt colored paper pipe cleaners

Once a group is gathered, we explain how the session came to be and give a short description of the life of Ada Lovelace. We then explore the etymology of the word *poem*, which derives from the Greek *poiesis*, meaning "to make." We have found it valuable for STEM-related audiences to hear that poets are, quite literally, *makers*.

After using Mali's Metaphor Dice as a way to generate some ideas to begin writing, we write together for seven to ten minutes. We then share what we wrote to begin to get ideas and written work into the room. A brief introduction to the micro:bit and the Hummingbird Bit follows, and then we ask participants to begin making a physical poem, or robot, or to return to their written work and begin to revise. Katie and Bud circulate through the room helping to solve problems, ask questions, and explore with participants. The workshops conclude with sharing what people made or wrote. In most cases, participants construct both a written poem and a made robot—but we cannot say with any certainty which text produced is the one participants would say they leave the workshop having completed. Some come to the workshops seeking to explore robotics tools. Others come because they like poems. A successful workshop for us is when people leave a little more confused about which is which.

As we turn to an analysis of how we see the texts, both robot and poem, functioning as primary and epitext, we will use the word *robot* to describe the physical composition of craft supplies animated and powered by the microcontroller. We will use the word *poem* to describe written text generated during our initial dice roll and thereafter revised by participants. This language is slippery, though. We struggle with whether we are creating robots or poems and which texts function in which ways. As Katie mentioned as we were drafting this chapter, "If someone is comfortable saying the phrase 'build a website' they should also be comfortable saying 'write a robot.'"

Taking Turns as Epitext

Throughout our workshops, we see robots and poems taking turns being the primary text of focus, and the companion text then seems to serve as an epitext. In the workshops, we see those texts functioning in four different ways. We turn our attention in this exploration to the author as audience for both the poems and the robots under construction. As the language of robot poems is slippery, so, too, are their place within the functions of epitext.

Production

As we have designed the workshop, both poem and robot are meant to serve as a draft of the other. A metaphor about brooms, described in writing, becomes a pair of popsicle arms whishing and wooshing, controlled by a motor attached to the microcontroller. But the moving arms may cause a fresh reflection on the words as written, and the author returns to them to make a change. This change suggests a tweak with the speed of the broom rotation, and so tinkering resumes on the robot. Both robot and poem become secondary to the other for a time—but both texts take turns.

Consider the role of code in this scenario and whether it functions as a primary text and whether it qualifies as peritext or epitext.

Considering the code used to program the robot may well add a third instance of text—or perhaps a second epitextual element of production—to this situation to consider. At the very least, it is poetic to ponder the notion that language is a tool used to make a tool work to produce a piece of poetry.

Reception

When workshop participants share their poems and robots, they receive feedback from other participants. Comments on the successful use of motion or light to produce effect might lead to confirmation of authorial intent or a recognition of a miss between desired and actual outcomes.

As the platform used to create these robots allows for quick adjustments, reception can be responded to in near-real time, with the authors making changes and revisions as they go. The texts, as well as readers in the room, contribute to a conversation that changes the texts themselves. Lather. Rinse. Repeat.

Extension

Extension is perhaps the slipperiest function of epitext for us to consider. In the context of our workshop, is a robot an extension of a poem, or is a poem an extension of a robot? Certainly, each draft and return to the other is a way of helping the creators understand the work they are creating better, and the poem might help a reader understand the reason a robot does what it does.

Binary Texts in Classrooms

Robots and poems are the chocolate and peanut butter of STEAM education. They belong together, especially in moments and experiences that transcend traditional subject matter boundaries. Creating other mashups of science and humanities is going to be essential for creating the society we would like to see: one thoughtfully approaching the adoption of new technologies that come with ethical and humane considerations as a part of the meaning construction process.

Frequently, the word *integration* is used to describe the juxtaposition of two disciplinary tools or stances within one classroom. Integration is seen as a way of mashing up different disciplines for the purposes of showing students how and why things might connect across classrooms and curriculum maps. Integration, though, is a loaded word that likely is not the right one to describe binary texts such as robot poems. Integration implies difference being pushed together— thoughtfully constructed, to be certain, but piecing together of differentness.

> How would you describe the relationship between the poem and the robot? Do you see one as primary and the other as secondary? Can they be considered to be one work?

Writing/composing/making/programming seem less different processes than elements of a larger human process of creation. Experiences that help dig deeper into these connections would serve our students well. The benefit of considering the function of epitext is that it can help students better understand how their texts speak to each other. It can, in the words of the science teacher who opened this chapter, help students to understand how composition can "feel this way."

Students are not asked to write or construct meaning in their studies often enough. When they are, the tasks often do not ask them to think deeply enough. Binary creation experiences like robot poems seem a way to address this problem. Creating experiences where multiple text creation is a focus will help to build the thoughtful poets, roboticists, and poetic roboticists we need.

Teachers and librarians wishing to try these activities with students can do so without expensive tools or supplies. It is possible to invite students to make robot poems (or poem robots) using only free, web-based tools such as Scratch (https://scratch.mit.edu) or MakeCode https://www.microsoft.com/en-us/makecode). We do wonder, though, what changes without the physicality of a made thing standing beside the writing of code and verse. That said, students can code their robot as a digital animation or game in Scratch or use the free micro:bit simulator in MakeCode to prototype a poem. Taylor Mali's Metaphor Dice game can be replaced (or augmented) with free, Web-based idea generating tools such as Scholastic Story Starter (http://www.scholastic.com/teachers/story-starters/writing-prompts). Alternatively, the activity could be completely unplugged by coming up with a list of nouns, adjectives, and abstract concepts that students randomly put together. Write the words onto popsicle or craft sticks and ask the students to pick one stick of each category. Then, students can prototype their poem with found objects from a recycling bin. Make time for students to move back and forth between their two creations, to see how one speaks to, and inspires changes or further revision in, the other.

An additional extension might be to reach out to someone else in the community to borrow equipment or learn alongside their work with similar tools. Creating writing robot poem workshops across contexts may well serve to further enhance the experience.

Reflecting on Your Learning

Epitext related to the production, reception, and extension of texts can be very ephemeral, making them unlikely to be available to others. What kind of epitexts might exist related to the production of these poem robots/robot poems that might someday be discoverable? How might epitext increase awareness and understanding of poem robots/robot poems?

References

Emig, J. (1977). Writing as mode of learning. *College Composition and Communication*, 28(2): 122–128.

Genette, G. (1997). *Paratexts: Thresholds of interpretation*. Cambridge, UK: Cambridge University Press.

Jenkins, H. (2007, March). *Transmedia storytelling 101*. http://henryjenkins.org/blog/2007/03/transmedia_storytelling_101.html

Mali, T. (2019). *Metaphor dice*. http://metaphordice.com

Romano, T. (2000). *Blending genre, altering style: Writing multigenre papers*. Portsmouth, NH: Boynton/Cook.

Rosenblatt, L. (1980). What facts does this poem teach you? *Language Arts*, 57(4): 386–394.

Smagorinsky, P. (1995). Constructing meaning in the disciplines: Reconceptualizing writing across the curriculum as composing across the curriculum. *American Journal of Education*, 103(2): 160–184.

Index

About the Editors and Contributors

James Blasingame, PhD, is the executive director of the Assembly on Literature for Adolescents of the National Council of Teachers of English (ALAN) and has also been ALAN president and *The ALAN Review* co-editor. He is the author or co-author of *John Green: Teen Whisperer, Stephenie Meyer: Into Twilight, Using Mentor Texts: Middle School, Books That Don't Bore 'Em: Young Adult Literature for Today's Generation, Gary Paulsen* (Teen Reads: Student Companions to Young Adult Literature), *Teaching Writing in Middle and Secondary Schools*, and *They Rhymed with Their Boots On: A Teacher's Guide to Cowboy Poetry*. Before coming to Arizona State University in 2000, Blasingame spent 24 years in Colorado, Utah, Kansas, and his home state of Iowa, where he was a school bus driver, a high school teacher, a rural high school principal, and a college wrestling coach.

Luciana C. de Oliveira, PhD, is Associate Dean for Academic Affairs and Professor in the School of Education at Virginia Commonwealth University. Her research focuses on issues related to teaching multilingual learners at the K-12 level, including the role of language in learning the content areas and teacher education, advocacy, and social justice. Dr. de Oliveira was the first Latina to ever serve as president (2018–2019) of TESOL International Association.

Eric Federspiel is an instructional designer and former middle and high school English teacher. In his time in the classroom, he used comics and graphic novels extensively as a way to engage struggling readers and writers. He and co-author Luke Rodesiler previously collaborated on a chapter for *Comic Connections: Analyzing Hero and Identity*.

Melissa Gross is a professor in the School of Information at Florida State University and a past president of the Association for Library and Information Science Education (ALISE). She received her PhD in Library and Information Science from the University of California, Los Angeles in 1998, received the prestigious American Association of University Women Recognition Award for Emerging Scholars in 2001, and has published extensively in the areas of information-seeking behavior, information literacy, library program and service evaluation, and information resources for youth. She has authored, co-authored, or co-edited 12 books. She recently published, with co-editor Julia Skinner, *Underserved Patrons in University Libraries: Assisting Students Facing Trauma, Abuse, and Discrimination* (Libraries Unlimited, 2021).

Deborah Heiligman is the author of 32 books, most of them nonfiction. Her latest, *Torpedoed: The True Story of the World War II Sinking of "The Children's Ship"* (2019), garnered four starred reviews, won the SCBWI Golden Kite Award, and is a finalist for the YALSA Excellence in Nonfiction Award. *Vincent and Theo: The Van Gogh Brothers* (2017), won the YALSA Excellence in Nonfiction Award, the Boston Globe-Horn Book Award for nonfiction, the SCBWI Golden Kite Award for nonfiction, and an ALA Printz Honor. *Charles and Emma: The Darwins' Leap of Faith* (2009) won the inaugural YALSA Excellence in Nonfiction Award, and was a Printz Honor and a National Book Award finalist. *The Boy Who Loved Math: The Improbable Life of Paul Erdős* (2013) won the Cook Prize, the Anne Izard Storytelling Award, was a New York Times notable book, and is a perennial favorite in elementary schools, as is *From Caterpillar to Butterfly* (1996). For more information, please visit www.DeborahHeiligman.com.

Katie Henry is the Head of Partner Engagement for the Micro:bit Educational Foundation in North America. She regularly consults with cross-sector education stakeholders worldwide, supporting the localized development of educational programs, professional learning workshops, and instructional materials on the topics of physical computing and computer science education. Katie is a former classroom teacher, licensed as a principal and computer technology integrator.

Jonathan M. Hollister is an assistant professor in the Department of Library, Archives, and Information Studies at Pusan National University. His research focuses on the depictions and uses of digital literacy skills and social information behaviors in recreational, popular media. Please visit https://jonathanmhollister.com for more information.

Bud Hunt is the IT and Technical Services Manager for the Clearview Library District in northern Colorado, where he serves a highly committed team of librarians and support staff in their work to be of service to their community through access to information, tools, high-quality resources, and programming. His extensive experience in both pedagogy and technical systems helps him to build bridges between the educational and technological sides of educational institutions. Bud is a teacher-consultant with the Colorado State University Writing Project; a former co-editor of the "New Voices" column of *English Journal*, a publication of the National Council of Teachers of English; and a co-founder of Learning 2.0: A Colorado Conversation. Bud reads, writes, and worries about the future of reading and writing and teaching and learning at http://www.budtheteacher.com.

Loren Jones, PhD, is an assistant clinical professor in the Department of Teaching and Learning, Policy and Leadership in the College of Education at the University of Maryland, College Park. Her research focuses broadly on teaching multilingual learners in K-12 settings, with an emphasis on best practices for literacy and language instruction and teacher education.

W. Kyle Jones, EdD, is a coordinator in the office of Academies and Career & Technical Education in Gwinnett County Public Schools in Georgia. He earned his doctoral degree in English Education in 2017 from Kennesaw State University, and taught high-school English language arts for nine years. His research interests include student identity and agency, teaching with an ethic of caring, and literacy skill development across curricula. He is a co-curator of the Teacher Casebook project and co-host of the Re:Learned vlog. To learn more, visit https://wkylejones.com.

Sharon Kane is a professor in the School of Education at the State University of New York at Oswego, where she teaches literacy courses, English Methods, and Young Adult literature. Recent publications include *Literacy and Learning in the Content Areas: Enhancing Knowledge in the Disciplines, 4th Edition* (2019), and *Integrating Literature in the Disciplines: Enhancing Adolescent Learning and Literacy, 2nd Edition* (2020).

Don Latham is a professor in the School of Information at Florida State University. He has served as a board member of the Association for Library and Information Science Education (ALISE), a member of the Young Adult Library Services Association (YALSA) Research Committee and Research Journal Advisory Committee, and chair of the YALSA Excellence in Nonfiction Award Committee. He has published extensively in the areas of information literacy, information behavior of youth, and young adult literature. He is co-author, along with Melissa Gross, of *Young Adult Resources Today: Connecting Teens with Books, Music, Games, Movies, and More* (2014) and co-editor, along with Shelbie Witte and Melissa Gross, of *Literacy Engagement through Peritextual Analysis* (2019).

Zoe Leonarczyk is a doctoral student at Florida State University College of Communication & Information in Tallahassee, Florida. She has completed her Master's degree in Library and Information Science from the University of South Florida. Her library experience covers cataloging, training, supervising, and user services.

Margaret Mackey is professor emerita in the School of Library and Information Studies at the University of Alberta. She has published widely on the subject of young people's reading and their multimedia and digital literacies. Her most recent book is *One Child Reading: My Auto-Bibliography* (2016).

Brady Nash, a former high-school English teacher, is a doctoral student at The University of Texas at Austin. As a teacher, he has worked to incorporate multimodal literacy practices and students' out-of-school interests into English language arts curricula. His current research focuses on how digital and multimodal texts can support critical literacy education in secondary classroom settings.

Shanedra D. Nowell is an associate professor of Secondary Education at Oklahoma State University. She taught middle- and high-school social studies and journalism courses before moving into higher education. Her research interests and publications include work focused on social studies education, Holocaust education, media literacy education, and content area writing.

Luke Rodesiler, a former high-school English teacher, is an associate professor of secondary education at Purdue University Fort Wayne, where he teaches students enrolled in English methods, content-area reading, and educational technology courses. His research and scholarship have appeared in numerous journals, including *English Education*, *Journal of Adolescent & Adult Literacy*, and *English Journal*.

Tyler C. Sisco teaches English and sponsors the yearbook at Washington High School in Kansas City, Kansas. They hold bachelor's degrees in Theatre and Secondary English Education from Oklahoma State University. Sisco is working on their English Language Learner Certificate through a joint program between their district and Kansas State University. In their first year of teaching, 2018–2019, they received an Educator of the Year award for their school.

Sharon L. Smith, PhD, is an elementary teacher in Miami-Dade County Public Schools. She holds bachelor's degrees in Elementary Education and Spanish from Purdue University and a doctorate in Teaching and Learning from the University of Miami. Her research currently focuses on the application of critical, humanizing literacies in the elementary school context with a specific focus on honoring and sustaining the stories of diverse children.

S. R. Toliver (@SR_Toliver) is an assistant professor of literacy and secondary humanities at the University of Colorado Boulder. Her scholarship centers on the freedom dreams of Black youth and honors the historical legacy that Black imaginations have had and will have on activism and social change. Specifically, she focuses on representations of and responses to Black youth in speculative fiction texts to discuss the implications of erasing Black children from futuristic and imaginative contexts and to assist teachers in imagining how they can use speculative fiction as a means to center Black joy and Black dreams.

Shelbie Witte (@shelbiewitte) holds the Chuck and Kim Watson Endowed Chair in Education and Professor in Adolescent Literacy and English Education at Oklahoma State University, where she is the founding director of the Initiative for 21st Century Literacies Research and site director emeritus of the OSU Writing Project. She serves as editor (with Sara Kajder) of *Voices from the Middle*, NCTE's premiere middle-level journal. Witte has published extensively in the area of 21st-century literacies, most recently *Studying Gaming Literacies: Theories to Inform Classroom Practice* and *Playing with Teaching: Considerations for Implementing Gaming in the Classroom*, both with Brill Publishing; and *Writing Changes Everything: Middle-Level Kids Writing Themselves into the World*, with NCTE.